Contents

Tasty Hot Dogs Recipe

Cooking Time: 17 minutes

Servings: 2

Ingredients:

- hot dog buns - 2
- Dijon mustard - 1 tbsp.
- hot dogs - 2
- cheddar cheese - 2 tbsp.; grated

Directions:

1. Put some hot dogs in your preheated air fryer and cook them at a temperature of 390 °F for 5 minutes.
2. Cut the hot dogs into hot dog buns before spreading mustard and cheese on the buns.
3. Move all of it back to your air fryer and cook for another 2 minutes at a temperature of 390 0F.
4. Now you can serve for lunch.

Nutrition Values:

Calories: 211; Fat: 3; Fiber: 8; Carbs: 12; Protein: 4

Delicious Lentils Fritters Recipe

Cooking Time: 20 minutes

Servings: 2

Ingredients:

- yellow lentils - 1 cup; soaked in water for 1 hour and drained
- hot chili pepper - 1; chopped.
- ginger piece - 1-inch; grated
- Turmeric powder - 1/2 tsp.
- Gar-am masala - 1 tsp.
- Baking powder - 1 tsp.
- Olive oil - 2 tsp.
- water - 1/3 cup
- Cilantro - 1/2 cup; chopped
- Spinach - 1 ½ cup; chopped
- garlic cloves - 4; minced
- red onion - 3/4 cup; chopped
- Salt and black pepper to the taste
- Mint chutney for serving

Directions:

1. Mix lentils with chili pepper, ginger, turmeric, garam masala, baking powder, salt, pepper, olive oil, water, cilantro, spinach, onion and garlic in your blender.
2. Pulse well and shape some medium balls out of the mix gotten from the blender.

3. Put them all in your preheated air fryer at a temperature of 400 °F.
4. Cook for about 10 minutes.
5. Serve your veggie fritters with a side salad for lunch.

Nutrition Values:

Calories: 142; Fat: 2; Fiber: 8; Carbs: 12; Protein: 4

Stuffed Portobello Mushrooms Mix

Cooking Time: 30 minutes

Servings: 4

Ingredients:

- big Portobello mushroom caps - 4
- bread crumbs - 1/3 cup
- Rosemary - 1/4 tsp.; chopped.
- Olive oil - 1 tbsp.
- ricotta cheese - 1/4 cup
- Parmesan - 5 tbsp.; grated
- Spinach - 1 cup; torn

Directions:

1. Drizzle and rub some oil on the mushroom caps; then transfer them to your air fryer's basket
2. Cook them at of 350 °F for about 2 minutes.
3. Also, mix half of the parmesan with ricotta, spinach, rosemary and bread crumbs in a bowl and stir well.
4. Stuff some mix inside the mushroom and sprinkle the remaining parmesan as toppings.
5. Put them in your air fryer's basket once more and cook at a temperature of 350 °F for 10 minutes.
6. Place them among different plates
7. Serve with a side salad for lunch.

Nutrition Values:

Calories: 152; Fat: 4; Fiber: 7; Carbs: 9; Protein: 5

Mouthwatering Chicken Kabobs Mix

Cooking Time: 30 minutes

Servings: 2

Ingredients:

- chicken breasts - 2; skinless, boneless and roughly cubed
- orange bell peppers - 3; cut into squares
- honey - 1/4 cup
- soy sauce - 1/3 cup
- Cooking spray
- Mushrooms - 6; halved
- Salt and black pepper to the taste

Directions:

1. Mix the chicken with salt, pepper, honey, say sauce and add some cooking spray in a bowl and toss well.
2. Thread the chicken neatly, and bell peppers and mushrooms on skewers;
3. Put them in the air fryer and cook at a temperature of 338 °F, for 20 minutes.
4. Divide into different plates and serve for lunch.

Nutrition Values:

Calories: 261; Fat: 7; Fiber: 9; Carbs: 12; Protein: 6

Delicious Fajitas Recipe

Cooking Time: 20 minutes

Servings: 4

Ingredients:

- chicken breasts - 1 lb.; cut into strips
- Garlic powder - 1 tsp.
- Cumin - 1/4 tsp.; ground
- Chili powder - 1/2 tsp.
- green bell pepper - 1; sliced
- Yellow onion - 1; chopped.
- Lime juice - 1 tbsp.
- Coriander - 1/4 tsp.; ground
- red bell pepper - 1; sliced
- Salt and black pepper to the taste
- Cooking spray
- Tortillas - 4; warmed up
- Salsa for serving
- lettuce leaves - 1 cup; torn for serving
- Sour cream for serving

Directions:

1. Mix chicken with garlic powder, cumin, chili, salt, pepper, coriander, lime juice, red bell pepper, green bell pepper and onion in a bowl.
2. Toss well to coat and keep it aside for about 10 minutes before moving to your air fryer
3. Then, drizzle some cooking spray all over the mix.
4. Toss and cook at 400 °F, for 10 minutes.
5. Arrange tortillas on a working surface.
6. Divide the chicken mix, as well as some salsa, sour cream and lettuce.
7. Wrap and serve the food for lunch.

Nutrition Values:

Calories: 317; Fat: 6; Fiber: 8; Carbs: 14; Protein: 4

Fried Thai Salad Recipe

Cooking Time: 15 minutes

Servings: 4

Ingredients:

- big shrimp - 12; cooked, peeled and de-veined
- Carrots - 1 cup; grated
- red cabbage - 1 cup; shredded
- A handful cilantro; chopped.
- small cucumber - 1; chopped.
- Lime Juice - 2 tsp
- Red curry paste - 2 tsp
- A pinch of salt and black pepper

Directions:

1. Mix cabbage with carrots, cucumber and shrimp.
2. Toss well to coat before introducing to your air fryer
3. Cook at a temperature of 360 °F for 5 minutes in the air fryer.
4. Add salt, pepper, cilantro, lime juice and red curry paste.
5. Toss once again and divide into different plates
6. Serve immediately.

Nutrition Values:

Calories: 172; Fat: 5; Fiber: 7; Carbs: 8; Protein: 5

Awesome Buttermilk Chicken Mix

Cooking Time: 28 minutes

Servings: 4

Ingredients:

- chicken thighs - 1 ½ lbs.
- buttermilk - 2 cups
- baking powder - 1 tbsp.
- sweet paprika - 1 tbsp.
- A pinch of cayenne pepper
- white flour - 2 cups
- Garlic powder - 1 tbsp.
- Salt and black pepper to the taste

Directions:

1. Mix chicken thighs with buttermilk, salt, pepper and cayenne in a bowl.
2. Toss to coat and keep it away for 6 hours.
3. Mix flour with paprika, baking powder and garlic powder in a separate bowl and stir gently.
4. Drain the chicken thighs, dip them in flour mix.

5. Place them in your air fryer and cook at 360 °F, for 8 minutes.

6. Then, flip the chicken pieces.

7. Cook them for another 10 minutes

8. Place them neatly on a platter and serve for lunch.

Nutrition Values:

Calories: 200; Fat: 3; Fiber: 9; Carbs: 14; Protein: 4

Succulent Turkey Breast Mix

Cooking Time: 57 minutes

Servings: 4

Ingredients:

- big turkey breast - 1
- Olive oil - 2 tsp.
- Smoked paprika - 1/2 tsp.
- Thyme - 1 tsp.; dried
- Sage - 1/2 tsp.; dried
- Mustard - 2 tbsp.
- maple syrup - 1/4 cup
- Butter - 1 tbsp.; soft
- Salt and black pepper to the taste

Directions:

1. Brush turkey breast with the olive oil; season with salt, pepper, thyme to taste.

2. Then add paprika and sage, and rub well.

3. Put them in your air fryer's basket and fry at a temperature of 350 °F, for 25 minutes.

4. Flip the turkey, then cook for another 10 minutes.

5. Flip once again and cook for extra 10 minutes.

6. Also, heat up a pan containing butter over medium heat, add mustard and maple syrup. Stir the mix well.

7. Cook for a couple of minutes and remove the heat.

8. Slice the turkey breast and divide into different plates

9. Serve with the maple glaze drizzled as toppings.

Nutrition Values:

Calories: 280; Fat: 2; Fiber: 7; Carbs: 16; Protein: 14

Special Gnocchi Recipe

Cooking Time: 27 minutes

Servings: 4

Ingredients:

- Parmesan - 1/4 cup; grated
- yellow onion - 1; chopped

- gnocchi - 16 oz.
- olive oil - 1 tbsp.
- garlic cloves - 3; minced
- spinach pesto - 8 oz.

Directions:

1. Grease your air fryer's pan with olive oil, add gnocchi, onion and garlic, and toss well to coat.
2. Place the pan in the air fryer and cook at a temperature of 400 °F for 10 minutes.
3. Add pesto, toss well to coat and cook for another 7 minutes at a temperature of 350 0F.
4. Divide into different plates and serve for lunch.

Nutrition Values:

Calories: 200; Fat: 4; Fiber: 4; Carbs: 12; Protein: 4

Tasty Hash Brown Toasts Recipe

Cooking Time: 17 minutes

Servings: 4

Ingredients:

- hash brown patties - 4; frozen
- Olive oil - 1 tbsp.
- Balsamic vinegar - 1 tbsp.
- Basil - 1 tbsp; chopped.
- Cherry tomatoes - 1/4 cup; chopped.
- Mozzarella - 3 tbsp.; shredded
- Parmesan - 2 tbsp; grated

Directions:

1. Put hash brown patties in your air fryer.
2. Then, drizzle some on the patties and cook them at a temperature of 400 °F for 7 minutes.
3. Mix the tomatoes with mozzarella, parmesan, vinegar and basil in a separate bowl and stir gently.
4. Cut the hash brown patties into different plates.
5. Top each plate with tomatoes mix
6. Now you can serve for lunch.

Nutrition Values:

Calories: 199; Fat: 3; Fiber: 8; Carbs: 12; Protein: 4

Indian Chickpeas

Preparation time: 10 minutes

Cooking Time: 25 minutes

Servings: 14

Ingredients:

- 6 cups canned chickpeas, drained
- 1 cup veggie stock

- 1 yellow onion, chopped
- 1 tablespoon ginger, grated
- 20 garlic cloves, minced
- 8 Thai peppers, chopped
- 2 tablespoons cumin, ground
- 2 tablespoons coriander, ground
- 1 tablespoons red chili powder
- 2 tablespoons garam masala
- 2 tablespoons vegan tamarind paste
- Juice of ½ lemon

Directions:

1. In your air fryer, mix chickpeas with stock, onion ginger, garlic, Thai peppers, cumin, coriander, chili powder, garam masala, tamarind paste and lemon juice, toss, cover and cook at 365 degrees F for 25 minutes.
2. Divide between plates and serve hot.
3. Enjoy!

Nutrition Values: calories 255, fat 5, fiber 14, carbs 16, protein 17

White Beans Stew

Preparation time: 10 minutes

Cooking Time: 20 minutes

Servings: 10

Ingredients:

- 2 pounds white beans, cooked
- 3 celery stalks, chopped
- 2 carrots, chopped
- 1 bay leaf
- 1 yellow onion, chopped
- 3 garlic cloves, minced
- 1 teaspoon rosemary, dried
- 1 teaspoon oregano, dried
- 1 teaspoon thyme, dried
- A drizzle of olive oil
- Salt and black pepper to the taste
- 28 ounces canned tomatoes, chopped
- 6 cups chard, chopped

Directions:

1. In your air fryer's pan, mix white beans with celery, carrots, bay leaf, onion, garlic, rosemary, oregano, thyme, oil, salt, pepper, tomatoes and chard, toss, cover and cook at 365 degrees F for 20 minutes.

2. Divide into bowls and serve.

3. Enjoy!

Nutrition Values: calories 341, fat 8, fiber 12, carbs 20, protein 6

Squash Bowls

Preparation time: 10 minutes

Cooking Time: 20 minutes

Servings: 5

Ingredients:

- 1 big butternut squash, peeled and roughly cubed
- 2 cups broccoli florets
- 1 tablespoon sesame seeds
- For the salad dressing:
- 1 and ½ tablespoon stevia
- 3 tablespoons wine vinegar
- 3 tablespoons olive oil
- 1 tablespoon coconut aminos
- 1 tablespoon ginger, grated
- 2 garlic cloves, minced
- 1 teaspoon sesame oil

Directions:

1. In your blender, mix stevia with vinegar, oil, aminos, ginger, garlic and sesame oil, pulse really well and leave aside for now.

2. In your air fryer, mix squash with the dressing you've made, broccoli and sesame seeds, toss, cover and cook at 370 degrees F for 20 minutes.

3. Divide salad into bowls and serve.

Enjoy!

Nutrition Values: calories 250, fat 4, fiber 6, carbs 26, protein 6

Cauliflower Stew

Preparation time: 10 minutes

Cooking Time: 15 minutes

Servings: 4

Ingredients:

- 30 ounces canned cannellini beans, drained
- 4 cups cauliflower florets
- 1 yellow onion, chopped
- 28 ounces canned tomatoes and juice
- 4 ounces canned roasted green chilies, chopped
- ½ cup hot sauce

- 1 tablespoon stevia
- 2 teaspoons cumin, ground
- 1 tablespoon chili powder
- A pinch of salt and cayenne pepper

Directions:

1. In your air fryer's pan, mix cannellini beans with cauliflower, onion, tomatoes and juice, roasted green chilies, hot sauce, stevia, cumin, chili powder, salt and cayenne pepper, stir, cover and cook at 360 degrees F for 15 minutes.
2. Divide into bowls and serve hot.

Enjoy!

Nutrition Values: calories 314, fat 6, fiber 6, carbs 29, protein 5

Simple Quinoa Stew

Preparation time: 10 minutes

Cooking Time: 15 minutes

Servings: 6

Ingredients:

- ½ cup quinoa
- 30 ounces canned black beans, drained
- 28 ounces canned tomatoes, chopped
- 1 green bell pepper, chopped
- 1 yellow onion, chopped
- 2 sweet potatoes, cubed
- 1 tablespoon chili powder
- 2 tablespoons cocoa powder
- 2 teaspoons cumin, ground
- Salt and black pepper to the taste
- ¼ teaspoon smoked paprika

Directions:

1. In your air fryer, mix quinoa, black beans, tomatoes, bell pepper, onion, sweet potatoes, chili powder, cocoa, cumin, paprika, salt and pepper, stir, cover and cook on High for 6 hours.
2. Divide into bowls and serve hot.

Enjoy!

Nutrition Values: calories 342, fat 6, fiber 7, carbs 18, protein 4

Green Beans Mix

Preparation time: 10 minutes

Cooking Time: 12 minutes

Servings: 4

Ingredients:

- 1 pound green beans

- 1 yellow onion, chopped
- 4 carrots, chopped
- 4 garlic cloves, minced
- 1 tablespoon thyme, chopped
- 3 tablespoons tomato paste
- Salt and black pepper to the taste

Directions:

1. In your air fryer's pan, mix green beans with onion, carrots, garlic, tomato paste,, salt and pepper, stir, cover and cook at 365 degrees F for 12 minutes.
2. Add thyme, stir, divide between plates and serve.

Enjoy!

Nutrition Values: calories 231, fat 4, fiber 6, carbs 7, protein 5

Chickpeas and Lentils Mix

Preparation time: 10 minutes

Cooking Time: 15 minutes

Servings: 6

Ingredients:

- 1 yellow onion, chopped
- 1 tablespoon olive oil
- 1 tablespoon garlic, minced
- 1 teaspoons sweet paprika
- 1 teaspoon smoked paprika
- Salt and black pepper to the taste
- 1 cup red lentils, boiled
- 15 ounces canned chickpeas, drained
- 29 ounces canned tomatoes and juice

Directions:

1. In your air fryer, mix onion with oil, garlic, sweet and smoked paprika, salt, pepper, lentils, chickpeas and tomatoes, stir, cover and cook at 360 degrees F for 15 minutes.
2. Ladle into bowls and serve hot.

Enjoy!

Nutrition Values: calories 341, fat 5, fiber 8, carbs 19, protein 7

Creamy Corn

Preparation time: 10 minutes

Cooking Time: 15 minutes

Servings: 6

Ingredients:

- 1 yellow onion, chopped
- A drizzle of olive oil

- 1 red bell pepper, chopped
- 3 cups gold potatoes, chopped
- 4 cups corn
- 2 tablespoons tomato paste
- ½ teaspoon smoked paprika
- 1 teaspoon cumin, ground
- Salt and black pepper to the taste
- ½ cup almond milk
- 2 scallions, chopped

Directions:

1. In your air fryer, mix onion with the oil, bell pepper, potatoes, corn, tomato paste, paprika, cumin, salt, pepper, scallions and almond milk, stir, cover and cook at 365 degrees F for 15 minutes.
2. Divide between plates and serve

Enjoy!

Nutrition Values: calories 312, fat 4, fiber 6, carbs 12, protein 4

Spinach and Lentils Mix

Preparation time: 10 minutes

Cooking Time: 15 minutes

Servings: 8

Ingredients:

- 10 ounces spinach
- 2 cups canned lentils, drained
- 1 tablespoon garlic, minced
- 15 ounces canned tomatoes, chopped
- 2 cups cauliflower florets
- 1 teaspoon ginger, grated
- 1 yellow onion, chopped
- 2 tablespoons curry paste
- ½ teaspoon cumin, ground
- ½ teaspoon coriander, ground
- 2 teaspoons stevia
- A pinch of salt and black pepper
- ¼ cup cilantro, chopped
- 1 tablespoon lime juice

Directions:

1. In a pan that fits your air fryer, mix spinach with lentils, garlic, tomatoes, cauliflower, ginger, onion, curry paste, cumin, coriander, stevia, salt, pepper and lime juice, stir, introduce in the fryer and cook at 370 degrees F for 15 minutes.
2. Add cilantro, stir, divide into bowls and serve.

Enjoy!

Nutrition Values: calories 265, fat 1, fiber 7, carbs 12, protein 7

Cajun Mushrooms and Beans

Preparation time: 10 minutes

Cooking Time: 15 minutes

Servings: 4

Ingredients:

- 2 tablespoons olive oil
- 1 green bell pepper, chopped
- 1 yellow onion, chopped
- 2 celery stalks, chopped
- 3 garlic cloves, minced
- 15 ounces canned tomatoes, chopped
- 8 ounces white mushrooms, sliced
- 15 ounces canned kidney beans, drained
- 1 zucchini, chopped
- 1 tablespoon Cajun seasoning
- Salt and black pepper to the taste

Directions:

1. In your air fryer's pan, mix oil with bell pepper, onion, celery, garlic, tomatoes, mushrooms, beans, zucchini, Cajun seasoning, salt and pepper, stir, cover and cook on at 370 degrees F for 15 minutes.
2. Divide veggie mix between plates and serve.

Enjoy!

Nutrition Values: calories 312, fat 4, fiber 7, carbs 19, protein 4

Eggplant Stew

Preparation time: 10 minutes

Cooking Time: 15 minutes

Servings: 4

Ingredients:

- 24 ounces canned tomatoes, chopped
- 1 red onion, chopped
- 2 red bell peppers, chopped
- 2 big eggplants, roughly chopped
- 1 tablespoon smoked paprika
- 2 teaspoons cumin, ground
- Salt and black pepper to the taste
- Juice of 1 lemon
- 1 tablespoons parsley, chopped

Directions:

1. In your air fryer's pan, mix tomatoes with onion, bell peppers, eggplant, smoked paprika, cumin, salt, pepper and lemon juice, stir, cover and cook at 365 degrees F for 15 minutes

2. Add parsley, stir, divide between plates and serve cold.

Enjoy!

Nutrition Values: calories 251, fat 4, fiber 6, carbs 14, protein 3

Corn and Cabbage Salad

Preparation time: 10 minutes

Cooking Time: 15 minutes

Servings: 4

Ingredients:

- 1 small yellow onion, chopped
- 1 tablespoon olive oil
- 2 garlic cloves, minced
- 1 and ½ cups mushrooms, sliced
- 3 teaspoons ginger, grated
- A pinch of salt and black pepper
- 2 cups corn
- 4 cups red cabbage, chopped
- 1 tablespoon nutritional yeast
- 2 teaspoons tomato paste
- 1 teaspoon coconut aminos
- 1 teaspoon sriracha sauce

Directions:

1. In your air fryer's pan, mix the oil with onion, garlic, mushrooms, ginger, salt, pepper, corn, cabbage, yeast and tomato paste, stir, cover and cook at 365 degrees F for 15 minutes

2. Add sriracha sauce and aminos, stir, divide between plates and serve.

Enjoy!

Nutrition Values: calories 360, fat 4, fiber 4, carbs 10, protein 4

Okra and Corn Mix

Preparation time: 10 minutes

Cooking Time: 15 minutes

Servings: 6

Ingredients:

- 1 green bell pepper, chopped
- 1 small yellow onion, chopped
- 3 garlic cloves, minced
- 16 ounces okra, sliced
- 2 cup corn

- 12 ounces canned tomatoes, crushed
- 1 and ½ teaspoon smoked paprika
- 1 teaspoon marjoram, dried
- 1 teaspoon thyme, dried
- 1 teaspoon oregano, dried
- Salt and black pepper to the taste

Directions:

1. In your air fryer, mix bell pepper with onion, garlic, okra, corn, tomatoes, smoked paprika, marjoram, thyme, oregano, salt and pepper, stir, cover and cook at 360 degrees F for 15 minutes.
2. Stir, divide between plates and serve.

Enjoy!

Nutrition Values: calories 243, fat 4, fiber 6, carbs 10, protein 3

Potato and Carrot Mix

Preparation time: 10 minutes

Cooking Time: 16 minutes

Servings: 6

Ingredients:

- 2 potatoes, cubed
- 3 pounds carrots, cubed
- 1 yellow onion, chopped
- Salt and black pepper to the taste
- 1 teaspoon thyme, dried
- 3 tablespoons coconut milk
- 2 teaspoons curry powder
- 3 tablespoons vegan cheese, crumbled
- 1 tablespoon parsley, chopped

Directions:

1. In your air fryer's pan, mix onion with potatoes, carrots, salt, pepper, thyme and curry powder, stir, cover and cook at 365 degrees F for 16 minutes.
2. Add coconut milk, sprinkle vegan cheese, divide between plates and serve.

Enjoy!

Nutrition Values: calories 241, fat 4, fiber 7, carbs 8, protein 4

Winter Green Beans

Preparation time: 10 minutes

Cooking Time: 16 minutes

Servings: 4

Ingredients:

- 1 and ½ cups yellow onion, chopped
- 1 pound green beans, halved
- 4 ounces canned tomatoes, chopped
- 4 garlic cloves, chopped
- 2 teaspoons oregano, dried
- 1 jalapeno, chopped
- Salt and black pepper to the taste
- 1 and ½ teaspoons cumin, ground
- 1 tablespoons olive oil

Directions:

1. Preheat your air fryer to 365 degrees F, add oil to the pan, also add onion, green beans, tomatoes, garlic, oregano, jalapeno, salt, pepper and cumin, cover and cook for 16 minutes.
2. Divide between plates and serve.

Enjoy!

Nutrition Values: calories 261, fat 5, fiber 8, carbs 10, protein 12

Green Beans Casserole

Preparation time: 10 minutes

Cooking Time: 20 minutes

Servings: 4

Ingredients:

- 1 teaspoon olive oil
- 2 red chilies, dried
- ¼ teaspoon fenugreek seeds
- ½ teaspoon black mustard seeds
- 10 curry leaves, chopped
- ½ cup red onion, chopped
- 3 garlic cloves, minced
- 2 teaspoons coriander powder
- 2 tomatoes, chopped
- 2 cups eggplant, chopped
- ½ teaspoon turmeric powder
- ½ cup green bell pepper, chopped
- A pinch of salt and black pepper
- 1 cup green beans, trimmed and halved
- 2 teaspoons tamarind paste
- 1 tablespoons cilantro, chopped

Directions:

1. In a baking dish that fits your air fryer, combine oil with chilies, fenugreek seeds, black mustard seeds, curry leaves, onion, coriander, tomatoes, eggplant, turmeric, green bell pepper, salt, pepper,

green beans, tamarind paste and cilantro, toss, put in your air fryer and cook at 365 degrees F for 20 minutes.

2. Divide between plates and serve.

Nutrition Values: calories 251, fat 5, fiber 4, carbs 8, protein 12

Chipotle Green Beans

Preparation time: 10 minutes

Cooking Time: 16 minutes

Servings: 6

Ingredients:

- 1 yellow onion, chopped
- 1 pound green beans, halved
- 2 teaspoons cumin, ground
- A drizzle of olive oil
- 12 ounces corn
- ¼ teaspoon chipotle powder
- 1 cup salsa

Directions:

1. In a pan that fits your air fryer, combine oil with onion, green beans, cumin, corn, chipotle powder and salsa, toss, introduce in your air fryer and cook at 365 degrees F for 16 minutes.
2. Divide between plates and serve.

Enjoy!

Nutrition Values: calories 224, fat 2, fiber 12, carbs 14, protein 10

Cranberry Beans Pasta

Preparation time: 10 minutes

Cooking Time: 15 minutes

Servings: 8

Ingredients:

- 2 cups canned cranberry beans, drained
- 2 celery ribs, chopped
- 1 yellow onion, chopped
- 7 garlic cloves, minced
- 1 teaspoon rosemary, chopped
- 26 ounces canned tomatoes, chopped
- ¼ teaspoon red pepper flakes
- 2 teaspoons oregano, dried
- 3 teaspoons basil, dried
- ½ teaspoon smoked paprika
- A pinch of salt and black pepper

- 10 ounces kale, roughly chopped
- 2 cups whole wheat vegan pasta, cooked

Directions:

1. In a pan that fits your air fryer, combine beans with celery, onion, garlic, rosemary, tomatoes, pepper flakes, oregano, basil, paprika, salt, pepper and kale, introduce in your air fryer and cook at 365 degrees F for 15 minutes.
2. Divide vegan pasta between plates, add cranberry mix on top and serve.

Enjoy!

Nutrition Values: calories 251, fat 2, fiber 12, carbs 12, protein 6

Mexican Casserole

Preparation time: 10 minutes

Cooking Time: 15 minutes

Servings: 4

Ingredients:

- 1 tablespoon olive oil
- 4 garlic cloves, minced
- 1 yellow onion, chopped
- 2 tablespoons cilantro, chopped
- 1 small red chili, chopped
- 2 teaspoons cumin, ground
- Salt and black pepper to the taste
- 1 teaspoon sweet paprika
- 1 teaspoon coriander seeds
- 1 pound sweet potatoes, cubed
- Juice of ½ lime
- 10 ounces green beans
- 2 cups tomatoes, chopped
- 1 tablespoon parsley, chopped

Directions:

1. Grease a pan that fits your air fryer with the oil, add garlic, onion, cilantro, red chili, cumin, salt, pepper, paprika, coriander, potatoes, lime juice, green beans and tomatoes, toss, place in your air fryer and cook at 365 degrees F for 15 minutes.
2. Add parsley, divide between plates and serve.

Enjoy!

Nutrition Values: calories 223, fat 5, fiber 4, carbs 7, protein 8

Endives and Rice Casserole

Preparation time: 10 minutes

Cooking Time: 20 minutes

Servings: 4

Ingredients:

- 1 tablespoon olive oil
- 2 scallions, chopped
- 3 garlic cloves chopped
- 1 tablespoon ginger, grated
- 1 teaspoon chili sauce
- A pinch of salt and black pepper
- ½ cup white rice
- 1 cup veggie stock
- 3 endives, trimmed and chopped

Directions:

1. Grease a pan that fits your air fryer with the oil, add scallions, garlic, ginger, chili sauce, salt, pepper, rice, stock and endives, place in your air fryer, cover and cook at 365 degrees F for 20 minutes.
2. Divide casserole between plates and serve.

Enjoy!

Nutrition Values: calories 220, fat 5, fiber 8, carbs 12, protein 6

Cabbage and Tomatoes

Preparation time: 10 minutes

Cooking Time: 12 minutes

Servings: 4

Ingredients:

- 1 tablespoon olive oil
- 1 green cabbage head, chopped
- Salt and black pepper to the taste
- 15 ounces canned tomatoes, chopped
- ½ cup yellow onion, chopped
- 2 teaspoons turmeric powder

Directions:

1. In a pan that fits your air fryer, combine oil with green cabbage, salt, pepper, tomatoes, onion and turmeric, place in your air fryer and cook at 365 degrees F for 12 minutes.
2. Divide between plates and serve.

Enjoy!

Nutrition Values: calories 202, fat 5, fiber 8, carbs 9, protein 10

Simple Endive Mix

Preparation time: 10 minutes

Cooking Time: 10 minutes

Servings: 4

Ingredients:

- 8 endives, trimmed
- Salt and black pepper to the taste
- 3 tablespoons olive oil
- Juice of ½ lemon
- 1 tablespoon tomato paste
- 2 tablespoons parsley, chopped
- 1 teaspoon stevia

Directions:

1. In a bowl, combine endives with salt, pepper, oil, lemon juice, tomato paste, parsley and stevia, toss, place endives in your air fryer's basket and cook at 365 degrees F for 10 minutes.
2. Divide between plates and serve.

Enjoy!

Nutrition Values: calories 160, fat 4, fiber 7, carbs 9, protein 4

Eggplant and Tomato Sauce

Preparation time: 10 minutes

Cooking Time: 12 minutes

Servings: 2

Ingredients:

- 4 cups eggplant, cubed
- 1 tablespoon olive oil
- 1 tablespoon garlic powder
- A pinch of salt and black pepper
- 3 garlic cloves, minced
- 1 cup tomato sauce

Directions:

1. In a pan that fits your air fryer, combine eggplant cubes with oil, garlic, salt, pepper, garlic powder and tomato sauce, toss, place in your air fryer and cook at 370 degrees F for 12 minutes.
2. Divide between plates and serve.

Enjoy!

Nutrition Values: calories 250, fat 7, fiber 5, carbs 10, protein 4

Brown Rice and Mung Beans Mix

Preparation time: 10 minutes

Cooking Time: 16 minutes

Servings: 2

Ingredients:

- ½ teaspoon olive oil
- ½ cup brown rice, cooked
- ½ cup mung beans
- ½ teaspoon cumin seeds

- ½ cup red onion, chopped
- 2 tomatoes, chopped
- 1 small ginger piece, grated
- 4 garlic cloves, minced
- 1 teaspoon coriander, ground
- ½ teaspoon turmeric powder
- A pinch of cayenne pepper
- ½ teaspoon garam masala
- 1 cup veggie stock
- Salt and black pepper to the taste
- 1 teaspoon lemon juice

Directions:

1. In your blender, mix tomato with garlic, onions, ginger, salt, pepper, garam masala, cayenne, coriander and turmeric and pulse really well.
2. In a pan that fits your air fryer, combine oil with blended tomato mix, mung beans, rice, stock, cumin and lemon juice, place in your air fryer and cook at 365 degrees F for 16 minutes.
3. Divide everything between plates and serve.

Enjoy!

Nutrition Values: calories 200, fat 6, fiber 7, carbs 10, protein 8

Lentils and Spinach Casserole

Preparation time: 10 minutes

Cooking Time: 16 minutes

Servings: 3

Ingredients:

- 1 teaspoon olive oil
- 1/3 cup canned brown lentils, drained
- 1 small ginger piece, grated
- 4 garlic cloves, minced
- 1 green chili pepper, chopped
- 2 tomatoes, chopped
- ½ teaspoon garam masala
- ½ teaspoon turmeric powder
- 2 potatoes, cubed
- Salt and black pepper to the taste
- ¼ teaspoon cardamom, ground
- ¼ teaspoon cinnamon powder
- 6 ounces spinach leaves

Directions:

1. In a pan that fits your air fryer combine oil with canned lentils, ginger, garlic, chili pepper, tomatoes, garam masala, turmeric, potatoes, salt, pepper, cardamom, cinnamon and spinach, toss, place in your air fryer and cook at 356 degrees F for 16 minutes.
2. Divide casserole between plates and serve.

Enjoy!

Nutrition Values: calories 250, fat 3, fiber 11, carbs 16, protein 10

Red Potatoes and Tasty Chutney

Preparation time: 10 minutes

Cooking Time: 14 minutes

Servings: 4

Ingredients:

- 2 pounds red potatoes, cubed
- 1 cup green beans
- 1 cup carrots, shredded
- 16 ounces canned chickpeas, drained
- 2 tablespoons olive oil
- 1 teaspoon coriander seeds
- 1 and ½ teaspoons cumin seeds
- 1 and ½ teaspoons garam masala
- ½ teaspoon mustard seeds
- 1 teaspoon garlic, minced
- For the chutney:
- ¼ cup water
- ½ cup mint
- ½ cup cilantro
- 1 small ginger piece, grated
- 2 teaspoons lime juice
- A pinch of salt

Directions:

1. In a baking dish that fits your air fryer, combine oil with potatoes, green beans, carrots, chickpeas, coriander, cumin, garam masala, mustard seeds and garlic, place in your air fryer and cook at 365 degrees F for 20 minutes.
2. In your blender, mix water with mint, cilantro, ginger, lime juice and salt and pulse really well.
3. Divide potato mix between plates, add mint chutney on top and serve.

Enjoy!

Nutrition Values: calories 241, fat 4, fiber 7, carbs 11, protein 6

Simple Veggie Salad

Preparation time: 10 minutes

Cooking Time: 10 minutes

Servings: 8

Ingredients:

- 1 and ½ cups tomatoes, chopped
- 3 cups eggplant, chopped
- 2 teaspoons capers
- Cooking spray
- 3 garlic cloves, minced
- 2 teaspoons balsamic vinegar
- 1 tablespoon basil, chopped
- A pinch of salt and black pepper

Directions:

1. Grease a pan that fits your air fryer with cooking spray, add tomatoes, eggplant, capers, garlic, salt and pepper, place in your air fryer and cook at 365 degrees F for 10 minutes.
2. Divide between plates, drizzle balsamic vinegar all over, sprinkle basil and serve cold.

Enjoy!

Nutrition Values: calories 171, fat 3, fiber 1, carbs 8, protein 12

SIDES

Pumpkin Ham Fritters

Preparation Time: 10 minutes

Servings: 4

INGREDIENTS

- 1 oz ham, chopped
- 1 cup dry pancake mix
- 1 egg
- 2 tbsp canned puree pumpkin
- 1 oz cheddar, shredded
- ½ tsp chili powder
- 3 tbsp of flour
- 1 oz beer
- 2 tbsp scallions, chopped

DIRECTIONS

1. Preheat the Air fryer to 370 F and in a bowl, mix the pancake mix and chili powder. Add the egg, puree pumpkin, beer, shredded cheddar, ham and scallions. Roll the mixture in 3 tbsp. of flour.
2. Arrange the balls into the basket and cook for 8 minutes. Drain on paper towel before serving.

Spicy Hot Crab Cakes

Preparation Time: 20 minutes

Servings: 6

Ingredients

- 1 lb. crab meat, shredded
- 2 eggs, beaten
- ½ cup breadcrumbs
- ⅓ cup finely chopped green onion
- ¼ cup parsley, chopped
- 1 tbsp mayonnaise
- 1 tsp sweet chili sauce
- ½ tsp paprika
- Salt and black pepper
- Olive oil to spray

Directions

1. In a bowl, add meat, eggs, crumbs, green onion, parsley, mayo, chili sauce, paprika, salt and black pepper; mix well with hands.
2. Shape into 6 cakes and grease them lightly with oil. Arrange them in the fryer, without overcrowding. Cook for 8 minutes at 400 F, turning once halfway through.

Pumpkin Wedges

Preparation Time: 30 minutes

Servings: 3

Ingredients

- ½ pumpkin, washed and cut into wedges
- 1 tbsp paprika
- 1 whole lime, squeezed
- 1 cup paleo dressing
- 1 tbsp balsamic vinegar
- Salt and pepper to taste
- 1 tsp turmeric

Directions

1. Preheat your Air Fryer to 360 F. Add the pumpkin wedges in your air fryer's cooking basket, and cook for 20 minutes. In a mixing bowl, mix lime juice, vinegar, turmeric, salt, pepper and paprika to form a marinade. Pour the marinade over pumpkin, and cook for 5 more minutes.

Potato Chips Creamy Dip

Preparation Time: 25 minutes

Servings: 3

INGREDIENTS

- 3 large potatoes
- 1 cup sour cream
- 2 scallions, white part minced
- 3 tbsp olive oil.

- ½ tsp lemon juice
- salt and black pepper

DIRECTIONS

1. Preheat the Air fryer to 350 F and slice the potatoes into thin slices; do not peel them. Soak them in water for 10 minutes, then dry them and spray with oil.
2. Fry the potato slices in two separate batches for 15 minutes; season with salt and pepper.
3. To prepare the dip, mix the sour cream, olive oil, the scallions, the lemon juice, salt and pepper.

Vegan Bok Choy Chips

Preparation Time: 10 minutes

Servings: 2

INGREDIENTS

- 2 tbsp olive oil
- 4 cups packed bok choy
- 1 tsp vegan seasoning
- 1 tbsp yeast flakes
- sea salt, to taste

DIRECTIONS

1. In a bowl, mix oil, bok choy, yeast and vegan seasoning. Dump the coated kale in the Air fryer's basket.
2. Set the temperature to 360 F and cook for to 5 minutes. Shake after 3 minutes.
3. Serve sprinkled with sea salt.

Veggie & Ham Rolls with Walnuts

Preparation Time: 15 minutes

Servings: 4

INGREDIENTS

- 8 rice leaves
- 4 carrots
- 4 slices ham
- 2 oz walnuts, finely chopped
- 1 zucchini
- 1 clove garlic
- 1 tbsp olive oil
- 1 tbsp ginger powder
- ¼ cup basil leaves, finely chopped
- salt and pepper

DIRECTIONS

1. In a cooking pan, pour olive oil and add the zucchini, carrots, garlic, ginger and salt; cook on low heat for 10 minutes.
2. Add the basil and walnuts, and keep stirring. Soak the rice leaves in warm water. Then fold one side above the filling and roll in.
3. Cook the rolls in the preheated Air fryer for 5 minutes at 300 F.

Rosemary Potato Chips

Preparation Time: 50 minutes

Servings: 3

Ingredients

- 3 whole potatoes, cut into thin slices
- ¼ cup olive oil
- 1 tbsp garlic
- ½ cup cream
- 2 tbsp rosemary

Directions

1. Preheat your Air Fryer to 390 F. In a bowl, add oil, garlic and salt to form a marinade. In a separate bowl, add potato slices and top with cold water. Allow sitting for 30 minutes. Drain the slices and transfer them to marinade.
2. Allow sitting for 30 minutes. Lay the potato slices onto your Air Fryer's cooking basket and cook for 20 minutes. After 10 minutes, give the chips a turn, sprinkle with rosemary and serve.

Simple Cheese Sandwich

Preparation Time: 20 minutes

Servings: 1

Ingredients

- 2 tbsp Parmesan, shredded
- 2 scallions
- 2 tbsp butter
- 2 slices bread
- ¾ cup Cheddar cheese

Directions

1. Preheat your Air Fryer to 360 F. Lay the bread slices on a flat surface. On one slice, spread the exposed side with butter, followed by cheddar and scallions. On the other slice, spread butter and then sprinkle cheese.
2. Bring the buttered sides together to form sand. Place the sandwich in your Air Fryer's cooking basket and cook for 10 minutes. Serve with berry sauce.

Cheesy Cheddar Biscuits

Preparation Time: 35 minutes

Servings: 8

Ingredients

- ½ cup + 1 tbsp butter
- 2 tbsp sugar
- 3 cups flour
- 1 ⅓ cups buttermilk
- ½ cup Cheddar, grated

Directions

1. Preheat your Air Fryer to 380 F. Lay a parchment paper on a baking plate. In a bowl, mix sugar, flour, ½ cup butter, cheese and buttermilk to form a batter. Make 8 balls from the batter and roll in flour.
2. Place the balls in your air fryer's cooking basket and flatten into biscuit shapes. Sprinkle cheese and the remaining butter on top. Cook for 30 minutes, tossing every 10 minutes. Serve warm.

Roasted Cashew Delight

Preparation Time: 20 minutes

Servings: 12

Ingredients

- 3 cups cashews
- 3 tbsp liquid smoke
- 2 tsp salt
- 2 tbsp molasses

Directions

1. Preheat your Air Fryer to 360 F. In a bowl, add salt, liquid, molasses, and cashews; toss to coat well. Place the coated cashews in your Air Fryer's cooking basket and cook for 10 minutes, shaking the basket every 5 minutes.

Hearty Grilled Ham and Cheese

Preparation Time: 15 minutes

Servings: 2

Ingredients

- 4 slices bread
- ¼ cup butter
- 2 slices ham
- 2 slices cheese

Directions

1. Preheat your Air Fryer to 360 degrees F. Place 2 bread slices on a flat surface. Spread butter on the exposed surfaces. Lay cheese and ham on two of the slices. Cover with the other 2 slices to form sandwiches. Place the sandwiches in the cooking basket and cook for 5 minutes.

Parsnip Fries

Preparation Time: 15 minutes

Servings: 3

INGREDIENTS

- 4 large parsnips
- ¼ cup flour
- ¼ cup olive oil
- ¼ cup water
- A pinch of salt

DIRECTIONS

1. Preheat the Air Fryer to 390 F and cut the parsnip to a half inch by 3 inches. In a bowl, mix the flour, olive oil, water, and parsnip. Mix well and coat. Line the fries in the Air fryer and cook for 15 minutes.
2. Serve with yogurt and garlic paste.

Tender Eggplant Fries

Preparation Time: 20 minutes **Servings:** 2

Ingredients

- 1 eggplant, sliced
- 1 tsp olive oil
- 1 tsp soy sauce
- Salt to taste

Directions

1. Preheat your Air Fryer to 400 F. Make a marinade of 1 tsp oil, soy sauce and salt. Mix well. Add in the eggplant slices and let stand for 5 minutes. Place the prepared eggplant slices in your Air Fryer's cooking basket and cook for 5 minutes. Serve with a drizzle of maple syrup.

Super Cabbage Canapes

Preparation Time: 15 minutes

Servings: 2

Ingredients

- 1 whole cabbage, washed and cut in rounds
- 1 cube Amul cheese
- ½ carrot, cubed
- ¼ onion, cubed
- ¼ capsicum, cubed
- Fresh basil to garnish

Directions

1. Preheat your Air Fryer to 360 F. Using a bowl, mix onion, carrot, capsicum and cheese. Toss to coat everything evenly. Add cabbage rounds to the Air Fryer's cooking basket.
2. Top with the veggie mixture and cook for 5 minutes. Serve with a garnish of fresh basil.

Crispy Bacon with Butterbean Dip

Preparation Time: 10 minutes

Servings: 2

Ingredients

- 1 -14 oz can butter beans
- 1 tbsp chives
- 3 ½ oz feta
- Pepper to taste
- 1 tsp olive oil
- 3 ½ oz bacon, sliced

Directions

1. Preheat your Air Fryer to 340 F. Blend beans, oil and pepper using a blender. Arrange bacon slices on your Air Fryer's cooking basket. Sprinkle chives on top and cook for 10 minutes. Add feta cheese to the butter bean blend and stir. Serve bacon with the dip.

Almond French Beans

Preparation Time: 25 minutes

Servings: 5

Ingredients

- 1 ½ pounds French beans, washed and drained
- 1 tbsp salt
- 1 tbsp pepper
- ½ pound shallots, chopped
- 3 tbsp olive oil
- ½ cup almonds, toasted

Directions

1. Preheat your Air Fryer to 400 F. Put a pan over medium heat, mix beans in hot water and oil until tender, about 5-6 minutes. Mix the boiled beans with oil, shallots, salt, and pepper. Add the mixture to your Air Fryer's cooking basket and cook for 20 minutes. Serve with almonds and enjoy!

Spicy Cajun Shrimp

Preparation Time: 15 minutes

Servings: 3

Ingredients

- ½ pound shrimp, sauce and deveined
- ½ tsp cajun seasoning
- Salt as needed
- 1 tbsp olive oil
- ¼ tsp pepper
- ¼ tsp paprika

Directions

1. Preheat your Air Fryer to 390 F. Using a bowl, make the marinade by mixing paprika, salt, pepper, oil and seasoning. Cut shrimp and cover with marinade. Place the prepared shrimp in your Air Fryer's cooking basket and cook for 10 minutes, flipping halfway through.

Roasted Brussels Sprouts

Preparation Time: 25 minutes

Servings: 4

Ingredients

- 1 block brussels sprouts
- ½ tsp garlic, chopped
- 2 tbsp olive oil
- ½ tsp pepper
- Salt to taste

Directions

1. Wash the Brussels thoroughly under cold water and trim off the outer leaves, keeping only the head of the sprouts. In a bowl, mix oil and garlic. Season with salt and pepper. Add prepared sprouts to this mixture and let rest for 5 minutes. Place the coated sprouts in your air fryer's cooking basket and cook for 15 minutes.

Buttery Shrimp Skewers

Cooking Time: 16 Minutes

Servings: 2

Ingredients:

- 8 shrimps; peeled and deveined
- 8 green bell pepper slices
- 1 tbsp. rosemary; chopped.
- 1 tbsp. butter; melted
- 4 garlic cloves; minced
- Salt and black pepper to the taste

Directions:

1. In a bowl; mix shrimp with garlic, butter, salt, pepper, rosemary and bell pepper slices; toss to coat and leave aside for 10 minutes.
2. Arrange 2 shrimp and 2 bell pepper slices on a skewer and repeat with the rest of the shrimp and bell pepper pieces.
3. Place them all in your air fryer's basket and cook at 360 °F, for 6 minutes. Divide among plates and serve right away.

Nutrition Values: Calories: 140; Fat: 1; Fiber: 12; Carbs: 15; Protein: 7

Fish and Couscous Recipe

Cooking Time: 25 Minutes

Servings: 4

Ingredients:

- 2½ lbs. sea bass; gutted
- 5 tsp. fennel seeds
- 3/4 cup whole wheat couscous; cooked
- 2 red onions; chopped
- Cooking spray
- 2 small fennel bulbs; cored and sliced
- 1/4 cup almonds; toasted and sliced
- Salt and black pepper to the taste

Directions:

1. Season fish with salt and pepper, spray with cooking spray; place in your air fryer and cook at 350 °F, for 10 minutes.
2. Meanwhile; spray a pan with some cooking oil and heat it up over medium heat.
3. Add fennel seeds to this pan; stir and toast them for 1 minute.
4. Add onion, salt, pepper, fennel bulbs, almonds and couscous; stir, cook for 2-3 minutes and divide among plates. Add fish next to couscous mix and serve right away.

Nutrition Values: Calories: 354; Fat: 7; Fiber: 10; Carbs: 20; Protein: 30

Delightful French Cod

Cooking Time: 32 Minutes

Servings: 4

Ingredients:

- 2 tbsp. olive oil
- 1 yellow onion; chopped
- 1/2 cup white wine
- 2 garlic cloves; minced
- 3 tbsp. parsley; chopped.
- 2 lbs. cod; boneless
- 14 oz. canned tomatoes; stewed
- Salt and black pepper to the taste
- 2 tbsp. butter

Directions:

1. Heat up a pan with the oil over medium heat, add garlic and onion; stir and cook for 5 minutes.
2. Add wine; stir and cook for 1 minute more.
3. Add tomatoes; stir, bring to a boil, cook for 2 minutes; add parsley; stir again and take off heat.
4. Pour this mix into a heat proof dish that fits your air fryer, add fish, season it with salt and pepper and cook in your fryer at 350 °F, for 14 minutes. Divide fish and tomatoes mix on plates and serve.

Nutrition Values: Calories: 231; Fat: 8; Fiber: 12; Carbs: 26; Protein: 14

Hawaiian Salmon Recipe

Cooking Time: 20 Minutes

Servings: 2

Ingredients:

- 20 oz. canned pineapple pieces and juice
- 2 medium salmon fillets; boneless
- 1/2 tsp. ginger; grated
- 2 tsp. garlic powder
- 1 tsp. onion powder
- 1 tbsp. balsamic vinegar
- Salt and black pepper to the taste

Directions:

1. Season salmon with garlic powder, onion powder, salt and black pepper, rub well, transfer to a heat proof dish that fits your air fryer, add ginger and pineapple chunks and toss them really gently.
2. Drizzle the vinegar all over, put in your air fryer and cook at 350 °F, for 10 minutes. Divide everything on plates and serve.

Nutrition Values: Calories: 200; Fat: 8; Fiber: 12; Carbs: 17; Protein: 20

Salmon and Avocado Sauce Recipe

Cooking Time: 20 Minutes

Servings: 4

Ingredients:

- 1 avocado; pitted, peeled and chopped
- 4 salmon fillets; boneless
- 1/4 cup cilantro; chopped
- 1/3 cup coconut milk
- 1 tbsp. lime juice
- 1 tbsp. lime zest; grated
- 1 tsp. onion powder
- 1 tsp. garlic powder
- Salt and black pepper to the taste

Directions:

1. Season salmon fillets with salt, black pepper and lime zest, rub well, put in your air fryer, cook at 350 °F, for 9 minutes; flipping once and divide among plates.
2. In your food processor, mix avocado with cilantro, garlic powder, onion powder, lime juice, salt, pepper and coconut milk; blend well, drizzle over salmon and serve right away.

Nutrition Values: Calories: 260; Fat: 7; Fiber: 20; Carbs: 28; Protein: 18

Tasty Catfish

Cooking Time: 30 Minutes

Servings: 4

Ingredients:

- 4 cat fish fillets
- A pinch of sweet paprika

- 1 tbsp. parsley; chopped
- 1 tbsp. lemon juice
- 1 tbsp. olive oil
- Salt and black pepper to the taste

Directions:

1. Season catfish fillets with salt, pepper, paprika, drizzle oil, rub well, place in your air fryer's basket and cook at 400 °F, for 20 minutes; flipping the fish after 10 minutes. Divide fish on plates, drizzle lemon juice all over, sprinkle parsley and serve.

Nutrition Values: Calories: 253; Fat: 6; Fiber: 12; Carbs: 26; Protein: 22

Salmon and Orange Marmalade Recipe

Cooking Time: 25 Minutes

Servings: 4

Ingredients:

- 1 lb. wild salmon; skinless, boneless and cubed
- 2 lemons; sliced
- 1/4 cup orange juice
- 1/3 cup orange marmalade
- 1/4 cup balsamic vinegar
- A pinch of salt and black pepper

Directions:

1. Heat up a pot with the vinegar over medium heat; add marmalade and orange juice; stir, bring to a simmer, cook for 1 minute and take off heat.
2. Thread salmon cubes and lemon slices on skewers, season with salt and black pepper, brush them with half of the orange marmalade mix, arrange in your air fryer's basket and cook at 360 °F, for 3 minutes on each side. Brush skewers with the rest of the vinegar mix; divide among plates and serve right away with a side salad.

Nutrition Values: Calories: 240; Fat: 9; Fiber: 12; Carbs: 14; Protein: 10

Salmon & Blackberry Glaze

Cooking Time: 43 Minutes

Servings: 4

Ingredients:

- 4 medium salmon fillets; skinless
- 1 cup water
- 1-inch ginger piece; grated
- Juice from 1/2 lemon
- 12 oz. blackberries
- 1 tbsp. olive oil
- 1/4 cup sugar
- Salt and black pepper to the taste

Directions:

1. Heat up a pot with the water over medium high heat, add ginger, lemon juice and blackberries; stir, bring to a boil, cook for 4-5 minutes; take off heat, strain into a bowl, return to pan and combine with sugar.
2. Stir this mix, bring to a simmer over medium low heat and cook for 20 minutes.
3. Leave blackberry sauce to cool down, brush salmon with it, season with salt and pepper, drizzle olive oil all over and rub fish well.
4. Place fish in your preheated air fryer at 350 °F and cook for 10 minutes; flipping fish fillets once. Divide among plates, drizzle some of the remaining blackberry sauce all over and serve.

Nutrition Values: Calories: 312; Fat: 4; Fiber: 9; Carbs: 19; Protein: 14

Stuffed Salmon Delight

Cooking Time: 30 Minutes

Servings: 2

Ingredients:

- 2 salmon fillets; skinless and boneless
- 5 oz. tiger shrimp; peeled, deveined and chopped
- 1 tbsp. olive oil
- 6 mushrooms; chopped.
- 3 green onions; chopped
- 2 cups spinach; torn
- 1/4 cup macadamia nuts; toasted and chopped
- Salt and black pepper to the taste

Directions:

1. Heat up a pan with half of the oil over medium high heat, add mushrooms, onions, salt and pepper; stir and cook for 4 minutes.
2. Add macadamia nuts, spinach and shrimp; stir, cook for 3 minutes and take off heat.
3. Make an incision lengthwise in each salmon fillet, season with salt and pepper, divide spinach and shrimp mix into incisions and rub with the rest of the olive oil.
4. Place in your air fryer's basket and cook at 360 °F and cook for 10 minutes; flipping halfway. Divide stuffed salmon on plates and serve.

Nutrition Values: Calories: 290; Fat: 15; Fiber: 3; Carbs: 12; Protein: 31

Honey Sea Bass Recipe

Cooking Time: 20 Minutes

Servings: 2

Ingredients:

- 2 sea bass fillets
- Zest from 1/2 orange; grated
- Juice from 1/2 orange
- 2 tbsp. mustard

- 2 tsp. honey
- 2 tbsp. olive oil
- 1/2 lb. canned lentils; drained
- A small bunch of dill; chopped
- 2 oz. watercress
- A small bunch of parsley; chopped
- A pinch of salt and black pepper

Directions:

1. Season fish fillets with salt and pepper, add orange zest and juice, rub with 1 tbsp. oil, with honey and mustard, rub, transfer to your air fryer and cook at 350 °F, for 10 minutes; flipping halfway.
2. Meanwhile; put lentils in a small pot, warm it up over medium heat, add the rest of the oil, watercress, dill and parsley; stir well and divide among plates. Add fish fillets and serve right away.

Nutrition Values: Calories: 212; Fat: 8; Fiber: 12; Carbs: 9; Protein: 17

Snapper Fillets and Veggies Recipe

Cooking Time: 24 Minutes

Servings: 2

Ingredients:

- 2 red snapper fillets; boneless
- 1 tbsp. olive oil
- 1/2 cup red bell pepper; chopped.
- 1/2 cup green bell pepper; chopped
- 1/2 cup leeks; chopped.
- 1 tsp. tarragon; dried
- A splash of white wine
- Salt and black pepper to the taste

Directions:

1. In a heat proof dish that fits your air fryer; mix fish fillets with salt, pepper, oil, green bell pepper, red bell pepper, leeks, tarragon and wine; toss well everything, introduce in preheated air fryer at 350 °F and cook for 14 minutes; flipping fish fillets halfway. Divide fish and veggies on plates and serve warm.

Nutrition Values: Calories: 300; Fat: 12; Fiber: 8; Carbs: 29; Protein: 12

Salmon Recipe

Cooking Time: 35 Minutes

Servings: 4

Ingredients:

- 1 lb. medium beets; sliced
- 1 ½ lbs. salmon fillets; skinless and boneless
- 6 tbsp. olive oil
- 1 tbsp. chives; chopped

- 1 tbsp. parsley; chopped.
- 1 tbsp. fresh tarragon; chopped
- 3 tbsp. shallots; chopped
- 1 tbsp. grated lemon zest
- 1/4 cup lemon juice
- 4 cups mixed baby greens
- Salt and pepper to the taste

Directions:

1. In a bowl; mix beets with 1/2 tbsp. oil and toss to coat.
2. Season them with salt and pepper, arrange them on a baking sheet; introduce in the oven at 450 °F and bake for 20 minutes.
3. Take beets out of the oven, add salmon on top, brush it with the rest if the oil and season with salt and pepper.
4. In a bowl; mix chives with parsley and tarragon and sprinkle 1 tbsp. of this mix over salmon.
5. Introduce in the oven again and bake for 15 minutes.
6. Meanwhile; in a boil with shallots with lemon peel, salt, pepper and lemon juice and the rest of the herbs mixture and stir gently.
7. Combine 2 tbsp. of shallots dressing with mixed greens and toss gently. Take salmon out of the oven, arrange on plates, add beets and greens on the side, drizzle the rest of the shallot dressing on top and serve right away.

Nutrition Values: Calories: 312; Fat: 2; Fiber: 2; Carbs: 2; Protein: 4

Black Cod & Plum Sauce

Cooking Time: 25 Minutes

Servings: 2

Ingredients:

- 2 medium black cod fillets; skinless and boneless
- 1 red plum; pitted and chopped
- 2 tsp. raw honey
- 1/4 tsp. black peppercorns; crushed
- 1 egg white
- 1/2 cup red quinoa; already cooked
- 2 tsp. whole wheat flour
- 4 tsp. lemon juice
- 1/2 tsp. smoked paprika
- 1 tsp. olive oil
- 2 tsp. parsley
- 1/4 cup water

Directions:

1. In a bowl; mix 1 tsp. lemon juice with egg white, flour and 1/4 tsp. paprika and whisk well.
2. Put quinoa in a bowl and mix it with ⅓ of egg white mix.

3. Put the fish into the bowl with the remaining egg white mix and toss to coat.

4. Dip fish in quinoa mix; coat well and leave aside for 10 minutes.

5. Heat up a pan with 1 tsp. oil over medium heat; add peppercorns, honey and plum; stir, bring to a simmer and cook for 1 minute.

6. Add the rest of the lemon juice, the rest of the paprika and the water; stir well and simmer for 5 minutes.

7. Add parsley; stir, take sauce off heat and leave aside for now.

8. Put fish in your air fryer and cook at 380 °F, for 10 minute. Arrange fish on plates, drizzle plum sauce on top and serve.

Nutrition Values: Calories: 324; Fat: 14; Fiber: 22; Carbs: 27; Protein: 22

Creamy Salmon Recipe

Cooking Time: 20 Minutes

Servings: 4

Ingredients:

- 4 salmon fillets; boneless
- 1/3 cup cheddar cheese; grated
- 1 ½ tsp. mustard
- 1/2 cup coconut cream
- 1 tbsp. olive oil
- Salt and black pepper to the taste

Directions:

1. Season salmon with salt and pepper, drizzle the oil and rub well.

2. In a bowl; mix coconut cream with cheddar, mustard, salt and pepper and stir well.

3. Transfer salmon to a pan that fits your air fryer; add coconut cream mix, introduce in your air fryer and cook at 320 °F, for 10 minutes. Divide among plates and serve.

Nutrition Values: Calories: 200; Fat: 6; Fiber: 14; Carbs: 17; Protein: 20

Spanish Salmon Recipe

Cooking Time: 25 Minutes

Servings: 6

Ingredients:

- 2 cups bread croutons
- 3 red onions; cut into medium wedges
- 5 tbsp. olive oil
- 6 medium salmon fillets; skinless and boneless
- 2 tbsp. parsley; chopped
- 3/4 cup green olives; pitted
- 3 red bell peppers; cut into medium wedges
- 1/2 tsp. smoked paprika
- Salt and black pepper to the taste

Directions:

1. In a heat proof dish that fits your air fryer, mix bread croutons with onion wedges, bell pepper ones, olives, salt, pepper, paprika and 3 tbsp. olive oil; toss well, place in your air fryer and cook at 356 °F, for 7 minutes.
2. Rub salmon with the rest of the oil; add over veggies and cook at 360 °F, for 8 minutes. Divide fish and veggie mix on plates, sprinkle parsley all over and serve.

Nutrition Values: Calories: 321; Fat: 8; Fiber: 14; Carbs: 27; Protein: 22

Flavored Jamaican Salmon Recipe

Cooking Time: 20 Minutes

Servings: 4

Ingredients:

- 4 cups baby arugula
- 2 cups radish; julienned
- 2 tsp. sriracha sauce
- 4 tsp. sugar
- 3 scallions; chopped
- 2 cups cabbage; shredded
- 1 ½ tsp. Jamaican jerk seasoning
- 1/4 cup pepitas; toasted
- 2 tsp. olive oil
- 4 tsp. apple cider vinegar
- 3 tsp. avocado oil
- 4 medium salmon fillets; boneless
- Salt and black pepper to the taste

Directions:

1. In a bowl; mix sriracha with sugar, whisk and transfer 2 tsp. to another bowl.
2. Combine 2 tsp. sriracha mix with the avocado oil, olive oil, vinegar, salt and pepper and whisk well.
3. Sprinkle jerk seasoning over salmon, rub with sriracha and sugar mix and season with salt and pepper.
4. Transfer to your air fryer and cook at 360 °F, for 10 minutes; flipping once.
5. In a bowl; mix radishes with cabbage, arugula, salt, pepper, sriracha and vinegar mix and toss well. Divide salmon and radish mix on plates, sprinkle pepitas and scallions on top and serve.

Nutrition Values: Calories: 290; Fat: 6; Fiber: 12; Carbs: 17; Protein: 10

Fried Branzino

Cooking Time: 20 Minutes

Servings: 4

Ingredients:

- 4 medium branzino fillets; boneless
- 1/2 cup parsley; chopped

- 2 tbsp. olive oil
- A pinch of red pepper flakes; crushed
- Zest from 1 lemon; grated
- Zest from 1 orange; grated
- Juice from 1/2 lemon
- Juice from 1/2 orange
- Salt and black pepper to the taste

Directions:

1. In a large bowl; mix fish fillets with lemon zest, orange zest, lemon juice, orange juice, salt, pepper, oil and pepper flakes; toss really well, transfer fillets to your preheated air fryer at 350 °F and bake for 10 minutes; flipping fillets once. Divide fish on plates, sprinkle with parsley and serve right away.

Nutrition Values: Calories: 261; Fat: 8; Fiber: 12; Carbs: 21; Protein: 12

Crusted Salmon Recipe

Cooking Time: 20 Minutes

Servings: 4

Ingredients:

- 1 cup pistachios; chopped.
- 4 salmon fillets
- 1/4 cup lemon juice
- 2 tbsp. honey
- 1 tbsp. mustard
- 1 tsp. dill; chopped
- Salt and black pepper to the taste

Directions:

1. In a bowl; mix pistachios with mustard, honey, lemon juice, salt, black pepper and dill; whisk and spread over salmon.
2. Put in your air fryer and cook at 350 °F, for 10 minutes. Divide among plates and serve with a side salad.

Nutrition Values: Calories: 300; Fat: 17; Fiber: 12; Carbs: 20; Protein: 22

Lemon Sole & Swiss Chard

Cooking Time: 24 Minutes

Servings: 4

Ingredients:

- 2 bunches Swiss chard; chopped
- 4 tbsp. butter
- 1/4 cup lemon juice

- 3 tbsp. capers
- 2 garlic cloves; minced
- 1 tsp. lemon zest; grated
- 4 white bread slices; quartered
- 1/4 cup walnuts; chopped.
- 1/4 cup parmesan; grated
- 4 tbsp. olive oil
- 4 sole fillets; boneless
- Salt and black pepper to the taste

Directions:

1. In your food processor, mix bread with walnuts, cheese and lemon zest and pulse well.
2. Add half of the olive oil, pulse really well again and leave aside for now.
3. Heat up a pan with the butter over medium heat, add lemon juice, salt, pepper and capers; stir well, add fish and toss it.
4. Transfer fish to your preheated air fryer's basket, top with bread mix you've made at the beginning and cook at 350 °F, for 14 minutes.
5. Meanwhile; heat up another pan with the rest of the oil, add garlic, Swiss chard, salt and pepper; stir gently, cook for 2 minutes and take off heat. Divide fish on plates and serve with sautéed chard on the side.

Nutrition Values: Calories: 321; Fat: 7; Fiber: 18; Carbs: 27; Protein: 12

Stuffed Calamari Recipe

Cooking Time: 35 Minutes

Servings: 4

Ingredients:

- 4 big calamari; tentacles separated and chopped and tubes reserved
- 2 tbsp. parsley; chopped.
- 2 oz. canned tomato puree
- 1 yellow onion; chopped
- 5 oz. kale; chopped
- 2 garlic cloves; minced
- 1 red bell pepper; chopped
- 1 tbsp. olive oil
- Salt and black pepper to the taste

Directions:

1. Heat up a pan with the oil over medium heat; add onion and garlic; stir and cook for 2 minutes.
2. Add bell pepper, tomato puree, calamari tentacles, kale, salt and pepper; stir, cook for 10 minutes and take off heat. stir and cook for 3 minutes.
3. Stuff calamari tubes with this mix, secure with toothpicks, put in your air fryer and cook at 360 °F, for 20 minutes. Divide calamari on plates; sprinkle parsley all over and serve.

Nutrition Values: Calories: 322; Fat: 10; Fiber: 14; Carbs: 14; Protein: 22

Swordfish and Mango Salsa

Cooking Time: 16 Minutes

Servings: 2

Ingredients:

- 2 medium swordfish steaks
- 2 tsp. avocado oil
- 1 tbsp. cilantro; chopped.
- 1 mango; chopped
- 1 avocado; pitted, peeled and chopped
- A pinch of cumin
- A pinch of onion powder
- A pinch of garlic powder
- 1 orange; peeled and sliced
- 1/2 tbsp. balsamic vinegar
- Salt and black pepper to the taste

Directions:

1. Season fish steaks with salt, pepper, garlic powder, onion powder and cumin and rub with half of the oil; place in your air fryer and cook at 360 °F, for 6 minutes; flipping halfway.
2. Meanwhile; in a bowl, mix avocado with mango, cilantro, balsamic vinegar, salt, pepper and the rest of the oil and stir well. Divide fish on plates; top with mango salsa and serve with orange slices on the side.

Nutrition Values: Calories: 200; Fat: 7; Fiber: 2; Carbs: 14; Protein: 14

Red Snapper Recipe

Cooking Time: 45 Minutes

Servings: 4

Ingredients:

- 1 big red snapper; cleaned and scored
- 3 garlic cloves; minced
- 1 jalapeno; chopped
- 1/4 lb. okra; chopped.
- 1 tbsp. butter
- 2 tbsp. olive oil
- 1 red bell pepper; chopped
- 2 tbsp. white wine
- 2 tbsp. parsley; chopped
- Salt and black pepper to the taste

Directions:

1. In a bowl; mix jalapeno, wine with garlic; stir well and rub snapper with this mix.
2. Season fish with salt and pepper and leave it aside for 30 minutes.

3. Meanwhile; heat up a pan with 1 tbsp. butter over medium heat, add bell pepper and okra; stir and cook for 5 minutes.
4. Stuff red snapper's belly with this mix; also add parsley and rub with the olive oil.
5. Place in preheated air fryer and cook at 400 °F, for 15 minutes; flipping the fish halfway. Divide among plates and serve.

Nutrition Values: Calories: 261; Fat: 7; Fiber: 18; Carbs: 28; Protein: 18

Tilapia & Chives Sauce

Cooking Time: 18 Minutes

Servings: 4

Ingredients:

- 4 medium tilapia fillets
- 2 tsp. honey
- 1/4 cup Greek yogurt
- Juice from 1 lemon
- 2 tbsp. chives; chopped
- Cooking spray
- Salt and black pepper to the taste

Directions:

1. Season fish with salt and pepper, spray with cooking spray, place in preheated air fryer 350 °F and cook for 8 minutes; flipping halfway.
2. Meanwhile; in a bowl, mix yogurt with honey, salt, pepper, chives and lemon juice and whisk really well. Divide air fryer fish on plates, drizzle yogurt sauce all over and serve right away.

Nutrition Values: Calories: 261; Fat: 8; Fiber: 18; Carbs: 24; Protein: 21

Chili Salmon Recipe

Cooking Time: 25 Minutes

Servings: 12

Ingredients:

- 1¼ cups coconut; shredded
- 1 lb. salmon; cubed
- 1/3 cup flour
- 4 red chilies; chopped
- 3 garlic cloves; minced
- 1/4 cup balsamic vinegar
- A pinch of salt and black pepper
- 1 egg
- 2 tbsp. olive oil
- 1/4 cup water
- 1/2 cup honey

Directions:

1. In a bowl; mix flour with a pinch of salt and stir.
2. In another bowl; mix egg with black pepper and whisk.
3. Put coconut in a third bowl.
4. Dip salmon cubes in flour, egg and coconut, put them in your air fryer's basket, cook at 370 °F, for 8 minutes; shaking halfway and divide among plates.
5. Heat up a pan with the water over medium high heat, add chilies, cloves, vinegar and honey; stir very well, bring to a boil, simmer for a couple of minutes; drizzle over salmon and serve.

Nutrition Values: Calories: 220; Fat: 12; Fiber: 2; Carbs: 14; Protein: 13

Salmon and Avocado Salad Recipe

Cooking Time: 30 Minutes

Servings: 4

Ingredients:

- 2 medium salmon fillets
- 1/4 cup melted butter
- 1 jalapeno pepper; chopped.
- 5 cilantro springs; chopped
- 2 tbsp. white wine vinegar
- 4 oz. mushrooms; sliced
- Sea salt and black pepper to the taste
- 12 cherry tomatoes; halved
- 2 tbsp. olive oil
- 8 oz. lettuce leaves; torn
- 1 avocado; pitted, peeled and cubed
- 1 oz. feta cheese; crumbled

Directions:

1. Place salmon on a lined baking sheet, brush with 2 tbsp. melted butter, season with salt and pepper; broil for 15 minutes over medium heat and then keep warm.
2. Meanwhile; heat up a pan with the rest of the butter over medium heat, add mushrooms; stir and cook for a few minutes.
3. Put tomatoes in a bowl, add salt, pepper and 1 tbsp. olive oil and toss to coat.
4. In a salad bowl; mix salmon with mushrooms, lettuce, avocado, tomatoes, jalapeno and cilantro. Add the rest of the oil, vinegar, salt and pepper, sprinkle cheese on top and serve.

Nutrition Values: Calories: 235; Fat: 6; Fiber: 8; Carbs: 19; Protein: 5

Salmon and Greek Yogurt Sauce Recipe

Cooking Time: 30 Minutes

Servings: 2

Ingredients:

- 2 medium salmon fillets
- 1 tbsp. basil; chopped

- 6 lemon slices
- 1 cup Greek yogurt
- 2 tsp. curry powder
- A pinch of cayenne pepper
- 1 garlic clove; minced
- 1/2 tsp. mint; chopped.
- 1/2 tsp. cilantro; chopped
- Sea salt and black pepper to the taste

Directions:

1. Place each salmon fillet on a parchment paper piece, make 3 splits in each and stuff them with basil.
2. Season with salt and pepper, top each fillet with 3 lemon slices, fold parchment, seal edges, introduce in the oven at 400 °F and bake for 20 minutes.
3. Meanwhile; in a bowl, mix yogurt with cayenne pepper, salt to the taste, garlic, curry, mint and cilantro and whisk well. Transfer fish to plates, drizzle the yogurt sauce you've just prepared on top and serve right away!

Nutrition Values: Calories: 242; Fat: 1; Fiber: 2; Carbs: 3; Protein: 3

Orange Marmalade Salmon

Preparation Time: 25 minutes

Servings: 4

Ingredients:

- Orange marmalade, 1/3 c.
- De-boned and cubed wild salmon, 1 lb.
- Black pepper.
- Balsamic vinegar, ¼ c.
- Orange juice, ¼ c.
- Sliced lemons,
- Salt.

Directions:

1. Set up pot with vinegar on fire to heat over medium heat.
2. Stir in orange juice and marmalade.
3. Allow to cook for 1 minute under reduced heat and remove from heat.
4. Arrange the lemon slices and salmon cubes on skewers.
5. Add seasonings and rub with half of the orange marmalade mix the place in the air fryer's basket.
6. Allow to cook for 3 minutes on each side at 3600F
7. Rub the skewers with the remaining vinegar mix.
8. Set on plates and serve immediately with a salad on the side.

Enjoy.

Nutrition Values:

Calories: 240, Fat: 9, Fiber: 12, Carbs: 14, Protein: 10

Salmon Delight and Avocado Sauce

Preparation Time: 20 minutes

Servings: 4

Ingredients:

- Garlic powder, 1 tsp.
- De-boned salmon fillets,
- Onion powder, 1 tsp.
- Grated lime zest, 1 tbsp.
- Salt.
- Black pepper.
- Chopped cilantro, ¼ c.
- Pitted and chopped avocado,
- Coconut milk, 1/3 c.
- Lime juice, 1 tbsp.

Directions:

1. Rub salmon fillets with lime zest and seasonings.
2. Transfer the salmon fillets into the air fryer.
3. Set the air fryer for 9 minutes at 3500F, allow to cook and flip once.
4. Have your food processor in place to process coconut milk, lime juice, cilantro, avocado, garlic powder, seasonings and onion powder until done.
5. Drizzle the mix over salmon to serve while still hot.

Enjoy.

Nutrition Values:

Calories: 260, Fat: 7, Fiber: 20, Carbs: 28, Protein: 18

Air-Fried Tilapia & Yoghurt Sauce

Preparation Time: 18 minutes

Servings: 4

Ingredients:

- Cooking spray
- Black pepper.
- Lemon juice, 1 lemon.
- Honey, 2 tsps.
- Chopped chives, 2 tbsps.
- Medium tilapia fillets,
- Greek yogurt, ¼ c.
- Salt.

Directions:

1. Add seasonings to fish then spray with cooking spray.

2. Transfer fish into the preheated air fryer to cook for 8 minutes at 3500 F and turn halfway.

3. In the meantime, set up a mixing bowl in place to combine chives, lemon juice, yogurt, honey and seasonings.

4. Plate the fish drizzled with yoghurt sauce and serve immediately.

Enjoy.

Nutrition Values:

Calories: 261, Fat: 8, Fiber: 18, Carbs: 24, Protein: 21

Rosemary Shrimp Skewers

Preparation Time: 16 minutes

Servings: 2

Ingredients:

- Minced garlic cloves,
- Green bell pepper slices,
- Black pepper.
- De veined shrimps,
- Chopped rosemary, 1 tbsp.
- Salt.
- Melted butter, 1 tbsp.

Directions:

1. Combine rosemary, butter, shrimp, garlic, bell pepper slices and seasonings in a medium bowl to coat evenly then reserve for 10 minutes.

2. Arrange 2 bell pepper slices and 2 shrimp on a skewer in that order

3. Do the same for the remaining bell pepper slices and shrimp and place them in the air fryer's basket.

4. Allow to cook for 6 minutes at 3600 F.

5. Set the shrimp skewers into plates and serve while still hot.

Enjoy.

Nutrition Values:

Calories: 140, Fat: 1, Fiber: 12, Carbs: 15, Protein: 7

Balsamic Swordfish and Mango Salsa

Preparation Time: 16 minutes

Servings: 2

Ingredients:

- Balsamic vinegar, ½ tbsp.
- Pitted and chopped avocado,
- Cumin.
- Garlic powder.
- Chopped mango,
- Black pepper.
- Medium swordfish steaks,

- Avocado oil, 2 tsps.
- Salt.
- Onion powder.
- Chopped cilantro, 1 tbsp.
- Peeled and sliced orange,

Directions:

1. Rub the seasonings, cumin, onion powder, garlic powder, and half of the oil to the fish steaks then place them in the air fryer.
2. Set the air fryer for 6 minutes at 3600F, allow to cook and flip halfway.
3. Combine vinegar, mango, balsamic, cilantro, seasonings and the remaining oil in a mixing bowl.
4. Set the fish into plates topped with mango salsa.
5. Serve with orange slices on the side.

Enjoy.

Nutrition Values:

Calories: 200, Fat: 7, Fiber: 2, Carbs: 14, Protein: 14

Crusted Air- Fryer Salmon

Preparation Time: 20 minutes

Servings: 4

Ingredients:

- Chopped dill, 1 tsp.
- Black pepper.
- Mustard, 1 tbsp.
- Chopped pistachios, 1 c.
- Salt.
- Honey, 2 tbsps.
- Salmon fillets,
- Lemon juice, ¼ c.

Directions:

1. Whisk together dill, pistachios, lemon juice, mustard, honey and seasonings in a mixing bowl.
2. Spread the combination over the salmon then put into the air fryer.
3. Allow to cook for 10 minutes at 3500F.
4. Serve the crusted salmon on plates with a side salad.

Enjoy.

Nutrition Values:

Calories: 300, Fat: 17, Fiber: 12, Carbs: 20, Protein: 22

Tasty Stuffed Salmon Delight

Preparation Time: 30 minutes

Servings: 2

Ingredients:

- Torn spinach, 2 c.
- Olive oil, 1 tbsp.
- Chopped mushrooms,
- Salt.
- De veined and chopped tiger shrimp, 5 oz.
- Toasted and chopped macadamia nuts, ¼ c.
- De-boned salmon fillets,
- Chopped green onions,
- Black pepper.

Directions:

1. Set a pan with half of the oil to heat up over medium high heat.
2. Fry the onions, mushroom and seasonings for 4 minutes.
3. Stir in spinach, shrimp and macadamia nuts, allow to cook for 3 minutes and remove from heat.
4. Make a slight cut on each salmon fillet then sprinkle some seasonings.
5. Set the shrimp and spinach into the cut then rub with the remaining olive oil and place in the air fryer's basket.
6. Allow to cook for 10 minutes at 3600F and flip halfway.
7. Divide the stuffed salmon on plates and serve.

Enjoy.

Nutrition Values:

Calories: 290, Fat: 15, Fiber: 3, Carbs: 12, Protein: 31

French Style Cod

Preparation Time: 32 minutes

Servings: 4

Ingredients:

- White wine, ½ c.
- De-boned cod, 2 lbs.
- Olive oil, 2 tbsps.
- Stewed canned tomatoes, 14 oz.
- Chopped yellow onion,
- Butter, 2 tbsps.
- Black pepper.
- Minced garlic cloves,
- Chopped parsley, 3 tbsps. .
- Salt.

Directions:

1. Set a pan with oil on fire to heat over medium heat.
2. Stir in onion and garlic to cook for 5 minutes.

3. Stir in wine to cook for 1 more minute.
4. Mix in tomatoes to boil for 2 minutes then stir in parsley and remove from heat.
5. Transfer the mix into a heat proof dish that fits the air fryer.
6. Add fish and season it with salt and pepper then cook for 14 minutes at 3500F.
7. Set the fish and tomatoes mix on plates and serve.

Nutrition Values:

Calories: 231, Fat: 8, Fiber: 12, Carbs: 26, Protein: 14

Simple Fish with Couscous

Preparation Time: 25 minutes

Servings: 4

Ingredients:

- Toasted and sliced almonds, ¼ c.
- Chopped red onions,
- Black pepper.
- Salt.
- Cored and sliced small fennel bulbs,
- Cooked whole wheat couscous, ¾ c.
- Gutted sea bass, 2½ lbs.
- Fennel seeds, 5 tsps.
- Cooking spray

Directions:

1. Sprinkle some pepper and salt to the fish then rub it with cooking spray and place in the air fryer.
2. Allow to cook for 10 minutes at 3500F.
3. Place a pan with cooking oil on fire to heat up over medium heat.
4. Stir in fennel seeds to cook for 1 minute.
5. Mix in fennel bulbs, couscous, almonds, onions and seasonings to cook for 3 minutes.
6. Plate the fish and couscous mix to serve.
7. Enjoy while still hot.

Nutrition Values:

Calories: 354, Fat: 7, Fiber: 10, Carbs: 20, Protein: 30

Flavored Salmon

Preparation Time: 1 hour 20 minutes

Servings: 6

Ingredients:

- Sliced lemon, 1
- Chopped tarragon, 1 tbsp.
- Salt.

- Whole salmon,
- Chopped dill, 1 tbsp.
- Black pepper.
- Lemon juice, 2 lemons.
- Minced garlic, 1 tbsp.

Directions:

1. Combine fish with lemon juice, salt, and pepper in a fish bowl to coat evenly.
2. Refrigerate for one hour.
3. Fill the salmon with lemon slices and garlic the place in the air fryer's basket.
4. Allow to cook for 25 minutes at 320 °F.
5. Serve on plates and with a tasty coleslaw on the side.

Nutrition Values:

Calories: 300, Fat: 8, Fiber: 9, Carbs: 19, Protein: 27

Air-Fried Stuffed Calamari

Preparation Time: 35 minutes

Servings: 4

Ingredients:

- Chopped red bell pepper,
- Chopped yellow onion,
- Minced garlic cloves,
- Black pepper.
- Chopped kale, 5 oz.
- Canned tomato puree, 2 oz.
- Big calamari,
- Chopped parsley, 2 tbsps.
- Olive oil, 1 tbsp.
- Salt.

Directions:

1. Set a pan with oil on fire to heat over medium heat.
2. Stir in garlic and onion to cook for 2 minutes.
3. Mix in calamari tentacles, bell pepper, tomato puree, kale and seasonings.
4. Allow to cook for 10 minutes and remove from heat.
5. Cook for 3 more minutes as you stir gently.
6. Fill the calamari tubes with the mix and hold with toothpicks then put into the air fryer.
7. Allow to cook for 20 minutes at 3600F.
8. Serve the calamari on plates sprinkled with parsley.

Enjoy.

Nutrition Values:

Calories: 322, Fat: 10, Fiber: 14, Carbs: 14, Protein: 22

Balsamic Catfish Fillets

Preparation Time: 22 minutes

Servings: 4

Ingredients:

- Minced garlic, ½ tsp.
- Worcestershire sauce, 4 oz.
- Black pepper.
- Butter, 2 oz.
- Balsamic vinegar, 1 tbsp.
- Jerk seasoning, ½ tsp.
- Mustard, 1 tsp.
- Chopped parsley, 1 tbsp.
- Catfish fillets,
- Cat sup, ¾ c.
- Salt.

Directions:

1. Set a pan on fire to melt the butter over medium heat.
2. Stir in jerk seasoning, cat sup, garlic, vinegar, seasonings and Worcestershire sauce then remove from heat.
3. Reserve for 10 minutes then drain and place into the preheated air fryer's basket.
4. Allow to cook for 10 minutes at 3500F as you shake the fillets halfway.
5. Serve the catfish fillets on plates topped with parsley.

Nutrition Values:

Calories: 351, Fat: 8, Fiber: 16, Carbs: 27, Protein: 17

Jamaican Style Salmon

Preparation Time: 20 minutes

Servings: 4

Ingredients:

- Jamaican jerk seasoning, 1 ½ tsps.
- Shredded cabbage, 2 c.
- Sriracha sauce, 2 tsps.
- Avocado oil, 3 tsps.
- Apple cider vinegar, 4 tsps.
- Black pepper.
- Baby arugula, 4 c.
- Julienned radish, 2 c.
- Sugar, 4 tsps.
- Chopped scallions,

- De-boned medium salmon fillets,
- Salt.
- Toasted pepitas, ¼ c.
- Olive oil, 2 tsps.

Directions:

1. Whisk together sugar and sriracha in a mixing bowl and set 2 tsps of the mix in a bowl.
2. Mix 2 tsps of sriracha mix with olive oil, avocado oil, vinegar and seasonings.
3. Season the salmon with jerk seasoning, brush with sugar mix and sriracha then sprinkle with some pepper and salt
4. Gently place the salmon into the air fryer.
5. Allow to cook for 10 minutes at 3600F flipping once.
6. In the meantime, combine arugula, radishes, cabbage vinegar mix and sriracha in a mixing bowl
7. Serve the salmon and radish mix on plates topped with scallions and pepitas.

Enjoy.

Nutrition Values:

Calories: 290, Fat: 6, Fiber: 12, Carbs: 17, Protein: 10

Cubed Salmon Chili

Preparation Time: 25 minutes

Servings: 12

Ingredients:

- Olive oil, 2 tbsps.
- Black pepper.
- Chopped red chilies,
- Flour, 1/3 c.
- Egg,
- Water, ¼ c.
- Balsamic vinegar, ¼ c.
- Minced garlic cloves,
- Shredded coconut, 1¼ c.
- Honey, ½ c.
- Cubed salmon, 1 lb.
- Salt.

Directions:

1. Combine salt and flour in a mixing bowl.
2. Have another mixing bowl in place to combine black pepper and egg.
3. In a third bowl, put the coconut.
4. Pass the salmon cubes through flour, egg then coconut and place them into the air fryer.
5. Allow to cook for 8 minutes at 3700F and shake halfway.
6. Set the salmon cubes on plates.

7. Set a pan with water on fire to boil over medium high heat.

8. Stir in honey, vinegar, chilies and cloves to boil under low heat.

9. Drizzle the mix on salmon to serve.

Enjoy.

Nutrition Values:

Calories: 220, Fat: 12, Fiber: 2, Carbs: 14, Protein: 13

Hawaiian Style Salmon

Preparation Time: 20 minutes

Servings: 2

Ingredients:

- Balsamic vinegar, 1 tbsp.
- Grated ginger, ½ tsp.
- Salt.
- Onion powder, 1 tsp.
- De-boned medium salmon fillets,
- Canned pineapple pieces and juice, 20 oz.
- Garlic powder, 2 tsps.
- Black pepper.

Directions:

1. Rub the salmon with onion powder, salt, garlic powder, and black pepper.

2. Put the salmon in a heat proof dish that fits the air fryer.

3. Mix in pineapple chunks and ginger then drizzle vinegar all over.

4. Place in the air fryer to cook for 10 minutes at 3500F.

5. Serve the salmon on plates.

Enjoy.

Nutrition Values:

Calories: 200, Fat: 8, Fiber: 12, Carbs: 17, Protein: 20

Parmesan Pollock

Preparation Time: 25 minutes

Servings: 6

Ingredients:

- Melted butter, 2 tbsps.
- Cooking spray
- Black pepper.
- Grated parmesan, ¼ c.
- De-boned Pollock fillets,
- Salt.
- Sour cream, ½ c.

Directions:

1. Whisk together parmesan, sour cream, butter and seasonings in a mixing bowl.
2. Spray the fish with cooking spray then season with pepper and salt.
3. Rub the sour cream mix on one side of every Pollock fillet and set in a preheated air fryer.
4. Allow to cook for 15 minutes at 3200F.
5. Serve the Pollock fillets on plates with a salad as a side.

Enjoy.

Nutrition Values:

Calories: 300, Fat: 13, Fiber: 3, Carbs: 14, Protein: 44

Orange Branzino

Preparation Time: 20 minutes

Servings: 4

Ingredients:

- Crushed red pepper flakes.
- Lemon zest, ½ lemon.
- Black pepper.
- Orange zest, 1 grated orange.
- De-boned medium branzino fillets,
- Salt.
- Chopped parsley, ½ c.
- Olive oil, 2 tbsps.
- Lemon zest, 1 grated lemon.
- Orange zest, ½ orange.

Directions:

1. Combine orange juice and zest, pepper flakes, lemon juice and zest, oil, fish fillets and seasonings in a mixing bowl to coat evenly then set in a preheated air fryer.
2. Allow to bake for 10 minutes at 3500F as you flip the fillets once.
3. Serve the fish on plates topped with sprinkled parsley.
4. Enjoy while still hot.

Nutrition Values:

Calories: 261, Fat: 8, Fiber: 12, Carbs: 21, Protein: 12

Spanish Style Salmon

Preparation Time: 25 minutes

Servings: 6

Ingredients:

- Pitted green olives, ¾ c.
- Smoked paprika, ½ tsp.
- De-boned medium salmon fillets,

- Sliced red bell peppers,
- Chopped parsley, 2 tbsps.
- Salt.
- Olive oil, 5 tbsps.
- Black pepper.
- Bread croutons, 2 c.
- Sliced red onions,

Directions:

1. Select a heat proof dish that fits in the air fryer well.
2. Mix in olives, paprika, onion wedges, bread croutons, bell peppers, 3 tbsps olive oil and seasonings and place in the air fryer.
3. Allow to cook for 7 minutes at 3560F.
4. Brush the salmon with the remaining oil and place into the air fryer.
5. Let the salmon cook for 8 minutes at 3600F.
6. Transfer the fish and veggie mix on plates.
7. Top with parsley to serve.

Enjoy.

Nutrition Values:

Calories: 321, Fat: 8, Fiber: 14, Carbs: 27, Protein: 22

Mouthwatering Snapper Fillets and Veggies Mix

Preparation Time: 24 minutes

Servings: 2

Ingredients:

- Dried tarragon, 1 tsp.
- Chopped leeks, ½ c.
- De-boned red snapper fillets,
- Chopped green bell pepper, ½ c.
- Salt.
- White wine.
- Olive oil, 1 tbsp.
- Chopped red bell pepper, ½ c.
- Black pepper.

Directions:

1. Have a heat proof dish that fits well in the air fryer.
2. Add red bell pepper, fish fillets, oil, pepper, wine, tarragon, leeks, green bell pepper and salt then place in the air fryer.
3. Allow to cook for 14 minutes at 3500F.

4. Flip the fish fillets halfway to cook on both sides
5. Serve the fish on plates with veggies.
6. Enjoy while still hot.

Nutrition Values:

Calories: 300, Fat: 12, Fiber: 8, Carbs: 29, Protein: 12

Awesome Black Cod in Plum Sauce

Preparation Time: 25 minutes

Servings: 2

Ingredients:

- Water, ¼ c.
- Whole wheat flour, 2 tsps.
- Egg white,
- Olive oil, 1 tsp.
- De-boned medium black cod fillets,
- Pitted and chopped red plum,
- Smoked paprika, ½ tsp.
- Crushed black peppercorns, ¼ tsp.
- Raw honey, 2 tsps.
- Parsley, 2 tsps.
- Already cooked red quinoa, ½ c.
- Lemon juice, 4 tsps.

Directions:

1. Whisk together egg white, ¼ tbsp paprika and 1 tsp of lemon juice in a mixing bowl.
2. Mix ⅓ of egg white mix and quinoa in another bowl.
3. Mix the egg white mix and fish in another bowl to coat evenly.
4. Pass fish through the quinoa mix and reserve for 10 minutes.
5. Set a pan with 1 tsp oil on fire allow to heat up over medium heat.
6. Stir in honey, peppercorns and plums and cook under reduced heat for 1 minute.
7. Mix in the remaining paprika, water and the remaining lemon juice.
8. Allow to cook for 5 minutes under reduced heat.
9. Stir in parsley, remove from heat and reserve.
10. Introduce the fish into the air fryer to cook for 10 minutes at 3800F.
11. Serve the fish into plates topped with plum sauce.

Enjoy.

Nutrition Values:

Calories: 324, Fat: 14, Fiber: 22, Carbs: 27, Protein: 22

Air-Fried Red Snapper

Preparation Time: 45 minutes

Servings: 4

Ingredients:

- White wine, 2 tbsps.
- Olive oil, 2 tbsps.
- Chopped red bell pepper,
- Butter, 1 tbsp.
- Chopped okra, ¼ lb.
- Salt.
- Minced garlic cloves,
- Chopped jalapeno,
- Cleaned and scored big red snapper,
- Chopped parsley, 2 tbsps.
- Black pepper.

Directions:

1. Mix wine, garlic and jalapeno in a mixing bowl then brush the snapper with the mix.
2. Add seasonings to the fish and reserve for 30 minutes.
3. In the meantime, set a pan with 1 tbsp butter on fire to melt over medium heat.
4. Stir in okra and bell pepper to cook for 5 minutes.
5. Fill the snapper's belly with the mix then spread some parsley and olive oil on the fish then introduce to the air fryer.
6. Allow to cook for 15 minutes at 4000F, as you turn the fish halfway.
7. Serve the snapper while still hot.

Enjoy.

Nutrition Values:

Calories: 261, Fat: 7, Fiber: 18, Carbs: 28, Protein: 18

Avocado Salad with Baked Salmon

Preparation Time: 30 minutes

Servings: 4

Ingredients:

- Sliced mushrooms, 4 oz.
- Chopped cilantro springs,
- Olive oil, 2 tbsps.
- Sea salt.
- Halved cherry tomatoes, 1
- Chopped jalapeno pepper,
- Torn lettuce leaves, 8 oz.
- Pitted and cubed avocado,
- Medium salmon fillets,
- Melted butter, ¼ c.

- White wine vinegar, 2 tbsps.
- Crumbled feta cheese, 1 oz.
- Black pepper.

Directions:

1. Set the salmon on a lined baking tray then rub with 2 tbsps melted butter.
2. Add seasonings and then broil for 15 minutes over medium heat.
3. Have a pan on fire with the remaining butter to melt over medium heat.
4. Stir in mushrooms to cook for a few minutes.
5. Place the tomatoes in a bowl and add 1 tbsp olive oil and seasonings.
6. Mix tomatoes, lettuce, tomatoes, salmon, jalapeno, mushrooms, cilantro and avocado in a salad bowl.
7. Add the remaining oil, vinegar and seasonings.
8. Serve the salmon and avocado salad topped with cheese.

Enjoy.

Nutrition Values:

Calories: 235, Fat: 6, Fiber: 8, Carbs: 19, Protein: 5

Honey Glazed Sea Bass

Preparation Time: 20 minutes

Servings: 2

Ingredients:

- Chopped parsley.
- Olive oil, 2 tbsps.
- Mustard, 2 tbsps.
- Honey, 2 tsps.
- Black pepper.
- Orange juice, ½ orange.
- Watercress, 2 oz.
- Sea bass fillets,
- Salt.
- Chopped dill.
- Orange zest, ½ grated orange.
- Drained canned lentils, ½ lb.

Directions:

1. Add seasonings to the fish fillets followed by orange juice and zest.
2. Brush the fish fillets with mustard, honey and 1 tbsp olive oil and then put into the air fryer.
3. Allow to cook for 10 minutes at 3500F as you flip halfway.
4. In the meantime, put lentils into a small pot to warm up over medium heat and stir in watercress, the remaining oil, parsley, and dill.
5. Plate the lentil mixture with fish fillets and serve while still hot.

Enjoy.

Nutrition Values:

Calories: 212, Fat: 8, Fiber: 12, Carbs: 9, Protein: 17

Curried Salmon and Greek Yogurt Sauce

Preparation Time: 30 minutes

Servings: 2

Ingredients:

- Chopped cilantro, ½ tsp.
- Sea salt.
- Curry powder, 2 tsps.
- Minced garlic clove,
- Chopped mint, ½ tsp.
- Black pepper.
- Cayenne pepper.
- Lemon slices,
- Chopped basil, 1 tbsp.
- Medium salmon fillets,
- Greek yogurt, 1 c.

Directions:

1. Have a piece of parchment paper and place the salmon fillets on them.
2. Make small cuts in each of the salmon fillets and fill with basil.
3. Add seasonings and top each fish fillet with lemon slices.
4. Fold everything in the parchment and seal the edges and then put in the oven.
5. Allow to cook for 20 minutes at 4000F.
6. In the meantime, whisk together curry, cilantro, mint, garlic, cayenne pepper, yoghurt and salt.
7. Serve the fish on plates topped with yoghurt sauce mix.
8. Serve immediately and enjoy while still hot.

Nutrition Values:

Calories: 242, Fat: 1, Fiber: 2, Carbs: 3, Protein: 3

Tasty Air Fried Cod Mix

Cooking Time: 22 minutes

Servings: 4

Ingredients:

- cod fish - 2, 7 ounces each
- A drizzle of sesame oil
- Salt and black pepper to the taste
- water - 1 cup
- dark soy sauce - 1 tsp

- light soy sauce - 4 tbsp
- sugar - 1 tbsp
- olive oil - 3 tbsp
- ginger – 4 slices
- spring onions - 3, chopped
- coriander - 2 tbsp, chopped

Directions:

1. Season fish with salt and pepper to taste.
2. Drizzle sesame oil, rub well and leave aside for 10 minutes.
3. Add fish to your air fryer and cook at a temperature of 356 0F for 12 minutes.
4. Also, add heat to a pot containing water over medium-high heat.
5. Then add dark and light soy sauce as well as some sugar. Stir gently, bring to a simmer and remove the heat.
6. Heat up a pan containing the olive oil over medium heat.
7. Also, add some ginger and green onions, and stir gently.
8. Cook for some minutes before taking off from the heat source.
9. Divide the fish on different plates, top with ginger and green onions.
10. Drizzle soy sauce mix and sprinkle coriander
11. Serve immediately.

Enjoy!

Nutritions:

calories 300, fat 17, fiber 8, carbs 20, protein 22

Salmon Cakes

Preparation Time: 1 hr 15 minutes

Servings: 4

Ingredients

- 10 oz cooked salmon
- 14 oz boiled and mashed potatoes
- 2 oz flour
- A handful of capers
- A handful of chopped parsley
- 1 tsp olive oil
- zest of 1 lemon

Directions

1. Place the mashed potatoes in a large bowl and flake the salmon over. Stir in capers, parsley, and lemon zest. Shape small cakes out of the mixture. Dust them with flour and place in the fridge to set, for 1 hour. Preheat the air fryer to 350 degrees F. Brush the olive oil over the basket's bottom and add the cakes. Cook for 7 minutes.

Favorite Shrimp Risotto

Preparation Time: 25 minutes

Servings: 4

Ingredients

- 4 whole eggs, beaten
- Pinch salt
- ½ cup rice, cooked
- Cooking spray
- ½ cup baby spinach
- ½ cup Monterey Jack cheese , grated
- ½ cup shrimp, chopped and cooked

Directions

1. Preheat your Air fryer to 320 F, and in a small bowl, add eggs and season with salt and basil; stir until frothy. Spray baking pan with non-stick cooking spray. Add rice, spinach and shrimp to the pan.
2. Pour egg mixture over and garnish with cheese. Place the pan in the air fryer's basket and cook for 14-18 minutes until the frittata is puffed and golden brown. Serve immediately.

Tuna Patties

Preparation Time: 50 minutes

Servings: 2

Ingredients

- 5 oz of canned tuna
- 1 tsp lime juice
- 1 tsp paprika
- ¼ cup flour
- ½ cup milk
- 1 small onion, diced
- 2 eggs
- 1 tsp chili powder, optional
- ½ tsp salt

Directions

1. Place all ingredients in a bowl and mix well to combine. Make two large patties, or a few smaller ones, out of the mixture. Place them on a lined sheet and refrigerate for 30 minutes. Cook the patties for 7 minutes on each side at 350 F.

Chinese Garlic Shrimp

Preparation Time: 15 minutes

Servings: 5

Ingredients

- 1 ½ pound shrimp
- Juice of 1 lemon
- 1 tsp sugar
- 3 tbsp peanut oil
- 2 tbsp cornstarch
- 2 scallions, chopped
- ¼ tsp chinese powder
- Chopped chili to taste
- 1 tsp salt
- 4 garlic cloves
- 1 tsp pepper

Directions

1. Preheat the Air fryer to 370 F, and in a Ziploc bag, mix lemon juice, sugar, pepper, oil, cornstarch, powder, chinese powder and salt. Add in the shrimp and massage to coat evenly. Let sit for 10 minutes.
2. Add garlic cloves, scallions and chili to a pan, and fry for a few minutes over medium heat. Place the marinated shrimp, garlic, chili and scallions in your air fryer's basket and cook for 10 minutes, until nice and crispy.

Beautiful Calamari Rings

Preparation Time: 20 minutes

Servings: 5

Ingredients

- 12 oz frozen squid
- 1 large egg, beaten
- 1 cup all-purpose flour
- 1 tsp ground coriander seeds
- 1 tsp cayenne pepper
- ½ tsp pepper
- ½ tsp salt
- Lemon wedges, to garnish
- olive oil for spray

Directions

1. In a bowl, mix flour, ground pepper, paprika, cayenne pepper and salt. Dredge calamari in eggs, followed by the floured mixture. Preheat your Air Fryer to 390 F and cook them for 15 minutes, until golden brown. Do it in batches if needed to avoid overcrowding. Garnish with lemon wedges and enjoy!

Cajun-Rubbed Jumbo Shrimp

Preparation Time: 10 minutes

Servings: 2 to 3

Ingredients

- 1 lb jumbo shrimp
- Salt to taste
- ¼ tsp old bay seasoning
- ⅓ tsp smoked paprika
- ¼ tsp cayenne pepper
- 1 tbsp olive oil

Directions

1. Preheat the Air fryer to 390 degrees. In a bowl, add the shrimp, paprika, oil, salt, old bay seasoning, and cayenne pepper; mix well. Place the shrimp in the fryer, close and cook for 5 minutes. Serve with mayo and rice.

Asian Shrimp Medley

Preparation Time: 20 minutes

Servings: 4

Ingredients

- 1 pound shrimp
- 2 whole onions, chopped
- 3 tbsp butter
- 1 ½ tbsp sugar
- 2 tbsp soy sauce
- 2 cloves garlic, chopped
- 2 tsp lime juice
- 1 tsp ginger, chopped

Directions

1. Preheat your Air fryer to 340 F, and in a bowl, mix lime juice, soy sauce, ginger, garlic, sugar and butter.

2. Add the mixture to a frying pan and warm over medium heat. Add in the chopped onions, and cook for 1 minute until translucent. Pour the mixture over shrimp, toss well and set aside for 30 minutes. Then, place the mixture in the air fryer's basket and cook for 8 minutes.

Greek Style Fried Mussels

Preparation Time: 25 minutes

Servings: 4

Ingredients

- 4 pounds mussels
- 2 tbsp olive oil
- 1 cup white wine
- 2 tsp salt
- 2 bay leaves
- 1 tbsp pepper

- 1 ½ cup flour
- 1 tbsp fenugreek
- 2 tbsp vinegar
- 5 garlic cloves
- 4 bread slices
- ½ cup mixed nuts

Directions

1. Preheat the Air Fryer to 350 F. Add oil, garlic, vinegar, salt, nuts, fenugreek, pepper and bread to a food processor, and process until you obtain a creamy texture. Add bay leaves, wine, and mussels to a pan.
2. Bring to a boil over medium heat, lower heat to low and simmer the mixture until the mussels have opened up. Take the mussels out and drain; remove from shells. Add flour to the creamy mixture prepared before.
3. Cover the mussels with the sauce and cook them in your Air Fryer for 10 minutes. Serve with fenugreek to enjoy.

Fish Nuggets

Preparation Time: 20 minutes

Servings: 4

Ingredients

- 28 oz fish fillets
- Lemon juice to taste
- Salt and pepper to taste
- 1 tsp drilled dill
- 4 tbsp mayonnaise
- 1 whole egg, beaten
- 1 tbsp garlic powder
- 3 ½ oz breadcrumbs
- 1 tbsp paprika

Directions

1. Preheat your air fryer to 400 F, and season fish fillets with salt and pepper. In a bowl, mix beaten egg, lemon juice, and mayonnaise. In a separate bowl, mix breadcrumbs, paprika, dill, and garlic powder.
2. Dredge fillets in egg mixture and then the garlic-paprika mix; repeat until all fillets are prepared. Place the fillets in your Air Fryer's cooking basket and cook for 15 minutes. Serve and enjoy!

Lemony Salmon

Preparation Time: 20 minutes

Servings: 2

Ingredients

- 2 salmon fillets

- Cooking spray
- Salt, to taste
- Zest of a lemon

Directions

1. Spray the fillets with olive oil and rub them with salt and lemon zest. Line baking paper in your air fryer's basket to avoid sticking. Cook the fillets for 10 minutes at 360 F, turning once halfway through. Serve with steamed asparagus and a drizzle of lemon juice.

Alaskan Salmon with Parsley Sauce

Preparation Time: 30 minutes

Servings: 4

Ingredients

- For Salmon
- 4 Alaskan wild salmon fillets, 6 oz each
- 2 tsp olive oil
- A pinch of salt
- For Dill Sauce
- ½ cup heavy cream
- ½ cup milk
- A pinch of salt
- 2 tbsp chopped parsley

Directions

1. Preheat your Air fryer to 310 F, and in a mixing bowl, add salmon and drizzle 1 tsp of oil. Season with salt and pepper. Place the salmon in your Air Fryer's cooking basket and cook for 20-25 minutes, until tender and crispy.
2. In a bowl, mix milk, chopped parsley, salt, and whipped cream. Serve the salmon with the sauce.

Cod Fennel Platter

Preparation Time: 15 minutes

Servings: 4

Ingredients

- 2 black cod fillets
- Salt and pepper to taste
- 1 cup grapes, halved
- 1 small fennel bulb, sliced
- ½ cup pecans
- 2 tsp white balsamic vinegar
- 2 tbsp extra virgin olive oil

Directions

1. Preheat your Air fryer to 400 F, and season the fillets with salt and pepper; drizzle oil on top. Place the fillet in the air fryer basket and cook for 10 minutes; set the fish aside to cool. In a bowl, add

grapes, pecans, and fennels. Drizzle oil over the grape mixture, and season with salt and pepper. Add the mixture to the basket and cook for 3 minutes. Add balsamic vinegar and oil to the mixture, season with salt and pepper. Pour over the fish, and serve.

Trout & Onion Frittata

Preparation Time: 12 minutes

Servings: 6

Ingredients

- 2 tbsp olive oil
- 1 onion, sliced
- 1 egg, beaten
- 6 tbsp crème fraiche
- ½ tbsp horseradish sauce
- 2 trout fillet, hot and smoked
- A handful of fresh dill

Directions

1. Heat oil in a frying pan over medium heat. Add onion and stir-fry until tender; season the onions well. Preheat your Air fryer to 320 F, and in a bowl, mix egg, crème Fraiche, and horseradish. Add cooked onion and trout, and mix well. Place the mixture in your fryer's cooking basket and cook for 20 minutes. Serve and enjoy!

Sautéed Shrimp

Preparation Time: 10 minutes

Servings: 4

Ingredients

- 5-6 oz tiger shrimp, 12 to 16 pieces
- 1 tbsp olive oil
- ½ a tbsp old bay seasoning
- ¼ a tbsp cayenne pepper
- ¼ a tbsp smoked paprika
- A pinch of sea salt

Directions

1. Preheat the Air fryer to 380 F, and mix all ingredients in a large bowl. Coat the shrimp with a little bit of oil and spices. Place the shrimp in the Air fryer's basket and fry for 6-7 minutes. Serve with rice or salad.

Parsley Catfish Fillets

Preparation Time: 25 minutes

Servings: 4

Ingredients

- 4 catfish fillets, rinsed and dried
- ¼ cup seasoned fish fry

- 1 tbsp olive oil
- 1 tbsp parsley, chopped

Directions

1. Preheat your Air fryer to 400 F, and add seasoned fish fry, and fillets in a large Ziploc bag; massage well to coat. Place the fillets in your Air fryer's cooking basket and cook for 10 minutes. Flip the fish and cook for 2-3 more minutes. Top with parsley and serve.

Shrimp Bowl

Preparation Time: 15 minutes

Servings: 6

Ingredients

- 1 ¼ pound tiger shrimp
- ¼ tsp cayenne pepper
- ½ tsp old bay seasoning
- ¼ tsp smoked paprika
- A pinch of salt
- 1 tbsp olive oil

Directions

1. Preheat your Air fryer to 390 F, and in a bowl, mix all listed ingredients. Place the mixture in your air fryer's cooking basket and cook for 5 minutes. Serve with warm rice and a drizzle of lemon juice.

Air-Fried Seafood

Preparation Time: 15 minutes

Servings: 4

Ingredients

- 1 lb fresh scallops, mussels, fish fillets, prawns, shrimp
- 2 eggs, lightly beaten
- Salt and black pepper
- 1 cup breadcrumbs mixed with the zest of 1 lemon
- Cooking spray

Directions

1. Clean the seafood as needed. Dip each piece into the egg; and season with salt and pepper. Coat in the crumbs and spray with oil. Arrange into your air fryer and cook for 6 minutes at 400 F, turning once halfway through.

Easy Crab Legs

Preparation Time: 15 minutes

Servings: 3

Ingredients

- 3 pounds crab legs

- 2 cups butter
- 1 cup salted water

Directions

1. Preheat the Air fryer to 380 F, and dip the crab legs in salted water; let stay for a few minutes. Place the crab legs in the basket and cook for 10 minutes. Melt the butter in a bowl in the microwave. Pour over crab legs to serve.

Air Fried Cod Fish

Preparation Time: 20 minutes

Servings: 4

Ingredients

- 7 ¼ oz codfish fillets
- 4 tbsp chopped cilantro
- Salt to taste
- A handful of green onions, chopped
- 1 cup water
- 5 slices of ginger
- 5 tbsp light soy sauce
- 3 tbsp oil
- 1 tsp dark soy sauce
- 5 cubes rock sugar

Directions

1. Preheat your Air fryer to 360 F, and cover codfish with salt and coriander; drizzle with oil. Place the fish fillet in your air fryer's cooking basket and cook for 15 minutes. Place the remaining ingredients in a frying pan over medium heat; cook for 5 minutes. Serve the fish with the sauce, and enjoy.

Fish & Cheese

Preparation Time: 15 minutes

Servings: 6

Ingredients

- 1 Bunch of basil
- 2 garlic cloves, minced
- 1 tbsp olive oil
- 1 tbsp Parmesan cheese , grated
- pepper and salt to taste
- 2 tbsp Pinenuts
- 6 white fish fillet
- 2 tbsp olive oil

Directions

1. Season the fillets with salt and pepper. Preheat the Air fryer to 350 F, and cook the fillets inside for 8 minutes.
2. In a bowl, add basil, oil, pine nuts, garlic and Parmesan; blend with your hand. Serve with the fish and enjoy!

Cilantro Catfish

Preparation Time: 20 minutes

Servings: 2

Ingredients

- 2 catfish fillets
- 2 tsp blackening seasoning
- Juice of 1 lime
- 2 tbsp butter, melted
- 1 garlic clove, mashed
- 2 tbsp cilantro

Directions

1. Preheat your Air fryer to 360 degrees F, and in a bowl, blend in garlic, lime juice, cilantro and butter. Divide the sauce into two parts, pour 1 part of the sauce over your fillets; cover the fillets with seasoning.
2. Place the fillets in your Air fryer's basket and cook for 15 minutes. Serve the cooked fish with remaining sauce.

Zesty Fishcakes

Preparation Time: 15 minutes

Servings: 2

Ingredients

- 8 oz salmon, cooked
- 1 ½ oz potatoes, mashed
- A handful of capers
- A handful of parsley, chopped
- Zest of 1 lemon
- 1 ¾ oz plain flour

Directions

1. Carefully flake the salmon. In a bowl, mix flaked salmon, zest, capers, dill, and mashed potatoes. Form small cakes using the mixture and dust the cakes with flour; refrigerate for 60 minutes. Preheat your Air Fryer to 350 and cook the cakes for 7 minutes. Serve chilled.

Parmesan Tilapia

Preparation Time: 15 minutes

Servings: 4

Ingredients

- ¾ cup grated Parmesan cheese

- 1 tbsp olive oil
- 2 tsp paprika
- 1 tbsp chopped parsley
- ¼ tsp garlic powder
- ¼ tsp salt
- 4 tilapia fillets

Directions

1. Preheat the Air fryer to 350 F, and mix parsley, Parmesan, garlic, salt, and paprika in a shallow bowl. Brush the olive oil over the fillets, and then coat them with the Parmesan mixture. Place the tilapia onto a lined baking sheet, and then into the Air fryer. Cook for 4 to 5 minutes on all sides.

Garlicky Prawns

Preparation Time: 1 h 15 minutes

Servings: 2

Ingredients

- 8 large prawns
- 3 garlic cloves, minced
- 1 rosemary sprig, chopped
- ½ tbsp melted butter
- Salt and pepper, to taste

Directions

1. Combine garlic, butter, rosemary, salt and pepper, in a bowl. Add the prawns to the bowl and mix to coat them well. Cover the bowl and refrigerate for an hour. Preheat the air fryer to 350 F, and cook for 6 minutes. Increase the temperature to 390 degrees, and cook for one more minute.

Tilapia with Old Bay Seasoning

Preparation Time: 15 minutes

Servings: 4

Ingredients

- 1 pound tilapia fillets
- 1 tbsp old bay seasoning
- 2 tbsp canola oil
- 2 tbsp lemon pepper
- Salt to taste
- 2-3 butter buds

Directions

1. Preheat your Fryer to 400 F, and drizzle oil over tilapia fillet. In a bowl, mix salt, lemon pepper, butter buds, and seasoning; spread on the fish. Place the fillets in the Air fryer and cook for 10 minutes, until tender and crispy.

Cajun Salmon with Parsley

Preparation Time: 10 minutes

Servings: 1

Ingredients

- 1 salmon fillet
- ¼ tsp brown sugar
- Juice of ½ lemon
- 1 tbsp cajun seasoning
- 2 lemon wedges
- 1 tbsp chopped parsley, for garnishing

Directions

1. Preheat the Air fryer to 350 F, and combine sugar and lemon; coat the salmon with this mixture. Coat with the Cajun seasoning as well. Place a parchment paper into the air fryer and cook the fish for 7 minutes. Serve with lemon wedges and chopped parsley.

Cod Cornflakes Nuggets

Preparation Time: 25 minutes

Servings: 4

Ingredients

- 1 ¼ lb cod fillets, cut into 4 to 6 chunks each
- ½ cup flour
- 1 egg
- 1 tbsp water
- 1 cup cornflakes
- 1 tbsp olive oil salt and pepper, to taste

Directions

1. Place the oil and cornflakes in a food processor and process until crumbed. Season the fish chunks with salt and pepper. In a bowl, beat the egg along with water. Dredge the chunks in flour first, then dip in the egg, and coat with cornflakes. Arrange on a lined sheet, and cook in the air fryer at 350 F for 15 minutes, until crispy.

Herbed Lobster

Preparation Time: 15 minutes

Servings: 3

Ingredients

- 4 oz lobster tails
- 1 tsp garlic, minced
- 1 tbsp butter
- Salt and pepper to taste
- ½ tbsp lemon Juice

Directions

1. Add all the ingredients to a food processor, except shrimp, and blend well. Wash lobster and halve using meat knife; clean the skin of the lobster and cover the lobster with the marinade. Preheat your Air fryer to 380 F.

2. Place the lobster in your Air Fryer's cooking basket and cook for 10 minutes. Serve with fresh herbs and enjoy!

Chicken Wings and Endives

Preparation Time: 40 minutes

Servings: 4

Ingredients:

- Halved chicken wings: 8
- Shaved endives: 6
- Olive oil: 1 tbsp
- Minced garlic cloves: 2
- White wine: ¼ cup
- Salt
- Black pepper
- Chopped rosemary: 1 tbsp
- Ground cumin: 1 tbsp

Directions:

1. Use salt, cumin, rosemary and black pepper to season the chicken wings, cook them in the air fryer for 10 minutes each side at 360 ˚F

2. Heat a greased pan over medium heat, add garlic, endives, salt, pepper, and the wine and let I simmer for 8 minutes

3. Spread it over the chicken and serve hot.

Nutrition Values:

Calories 270, fat 8, fiber 12, carbs 20, protein 22

Turkey and Parsley Pesto

Prep + Cooking Time:1hours and 10 minutes

Servings: 4

Ingredients:

- Chopped parsley: 1 cup
- Olive oil: ½ cup
- Red wine: ¼ cup
- Garlic cloves: 4
- Salt
- Black pepper
- Maple syrup: a drizzle
- Turkey breasts: 2 boneless, skinless and halved

Directions:

1. Mix the parsley, garlic, salt, pepper, oil, wine, and maple syrup in a blender and pulse it to make pesto. Place it in a bowl
2. Add turkey breasts into the bowl and toss. place it in the fridge for 30 minutes
3. While retaining the parsley pesto, drain the turkey breast
4. Cook in the air fryer for 35 minutes at 380°F; make sure to flip it after 17 minutes
5. Top it with parsley pesto and serve hot.

Nutrition Values:

Calories 274, fat 10, fiber 12, carbs 20, protein 17

Chicken Breasts and Veggies

Preparation Time: 30 minutes

Servings: 4

Ingredients:

- Chicken breast: 2 skinless and boneless
- Olive oil: 2 tbsp
- Chopped onions: 1
- Minced garlic cloves: 2
- Salt
- Black pepper
- Halved brown mushroom: 12
- Chopped red bell pepper: 1
- Roughly chopped green bell pepper: 1
- Shredded cheddar cheese: 2 tbsp

Directions:

1. Using salt and pepper, season the chicken breast. Rub it with garlic and 1 tbsp oil, cook each side for 6 minutes in the air fryer at 390 °F
2. Heat a greased pan over medium, heat. Add onions, stir and cook for 2 minutes. Add mushroom and bell pepper and cook for 6 minutes
3. Sprinkle it over the chicken and serve hot.

Nutrition Values:

Calories 285, fat 12, fiber 11, carbs 20, protein 22

Chicken and Green Coconut Sauce

Preparation Time: 26 minutes

Servings: 4

Ingredients:

- Roughly chopped green onions: 10
- Grated ginger: 1 tbsp
- Minced garlic cloves: 4
- Oyster sauce: 2 tbsp
- Soy sauce: 3 tbsp

- Chinese five spice: 1 tbsp
- Chicken Drumsticks: 10
- Coconut milk: 1 cup
- Salt
- Black pepper
- Olive oil: 1 tbsp
- Chopped parsley: ¼ cup
- Lemon juice: 1 tbsp

Directions:

1. Mix the green onions with the ginger, garlic, soy sauce, oyster sauce, five spices, salt, Pepper, oil, and coconut milk in a blender and whisk well
2. Mix the chicken and green sauce in a baking dish and toss it, cook in the air fryer for 16 minutes at 370°F
3. Top it with parsley and lemon juice then serve hot.

Nutrition Values:

Calories 281, fat 11, fiber 12, carbs 22, protein 16

Simple Chicken Thighs

Preparation Time: 26 minutes

Servings: 6

Ingredients:

- Chicken thigh: 8
- Turmeric powder: 1 tbsp
- Ground coriander: 1 tbsp
- Grated ginger: 1 tbsp
- Sweet paprika: 1 tbsp
- Salt
- Black pepper
- Olive oil: 2 tbsp
- Lime juice: 1 tbsp

Directions:

1. Toss all the ingredients in a bowl
2. Cook in the air fryer for 8 minutes each side at 370°F.then serve hot

Nutrition Values:

Calories 270, fat 11, fiber 11, carbs 17, protein 11

Chicken Breasts Delight

Preparation Time: 35 minutes

Servings: 6

Ingredients:

- Olive oil: 1 tbsp

- Chicken breasts: 3 ½ pounds
- Chicken stock: 1 cup
- Chopped yellow onions: 1 ¼ cup
- Lime juice: 1 tbsp
- Sweet paprika: 2 tbsp
- Red pepper flakes: 1 tbsp
- Chopped green onions: 2 tbsp
- Salt
- Black pepper

Directions:

1. Heat a greased pan over medium heat. Add onions, lime juice, paprika, green onions, pepper flakes, salt and pepper and stir. Cook for 8 minutes
2. Add chicken breasts and let it simmer for 1 minute
3. Transfer to the air fryer and cook for 12 minutes at 370°F. Then serve hot

Nutrition Values:

Calories 280, fat 11, fiber 13, carbs 27, protein 16

Tomato Chicken Mix

Preparation Time: 30 minutes

Servings: 6

Ingredients:

- Tomato sauce: 14 ounce
- Olive oil: 1 tbsp
- Chicken breast: 4 medium skinless and boneless
- Salt
- Black pepper'
- Dries oregano: 1 tbsp
- Grated mozzarella cheese: 6 ounces
- Garlic powder: 1 tbsp

Directions:

1. Use salt, pepper, garlic powder, and the oregano to season the chicken, cook in the air fryer for 5 minutes at 360 ° F. Transfer it to a greased pan. Add tomato sauce
2. Top it with mozzarella, cook for 15 minutes in the air fryer at 350 ° F. Serve hot

Nutrition Values:

Calories 270, fat 10, fiber 16, carbs 16, protein 18

Chicken and Veggies

Preparation Time: 35 minutes

Servings: 4

Ingredient:

- Chopped red onions: 1

- Chopped carrot: 1
- Minced garlic cloves: 3
- Chicken breast: 4 boneless and skinless
- Chopped celery stalk: 1
- Chicken stock: 1 cup
- Olive oil: 2 tbsp
- Dried rosemary: ½ tbsp
- Dried sage: 1 tbsp
- Salt
- Black pepper

Directions:

1. Take a pan and place all the ingredients in it then toss it well, cook for 25 minutes at 360 °F. Serve hot

Nutrition Values:

Calories 292, fat 12, fiber 16, carbs 19, protein 15

Japanese Chicken Thighs

Preparation Time: 40 minutes

Servings: 5

Ingredients:

- Chicken thighs: 2 pounds
- Salt
- Black pepper
- Chopped spring onions: 5
- Olive oil: 2 tbsp
- Sherry wine: 1 tbsp
- White vinegar: ½ tbsp
- Soy sauce: 1 tbsp
- Sugar: ¼ tbsp

Directions:

1. Using salt and pepper, season the chicken. Rub it with 1 tbsp oil and place it in the air fryer basket, cook for 10 minutes on each side in the air fryer in the air fryer at 360°F
2. Heat a greased pan over medium heat. Add spring onions, sherry wine, vinegar, soy sauce, and sugar and whisk it then let it cook for 10 minutes
3. Drizzle it over the chicken and serve hot.

Nutrition Values:

Calories 271, fat 8, fiber 12, carbs 26, protein 17

Air Fried Whole Chicken

Preparation Time: 30 minutes

Servings: 8

Ingredients:

- Whole chicken: 1 cut into medium pieces
- White wine: 3 tbsp
- Chopped carrots: 2
- Chicken stock: 1 cup
- Grated ginger: 1 tbsp
- Salt
- Black pepper

Directions:

1. Mix all the ingredients in a pan, cook for 20 minutes at 370°F. Serve hot

Nutrition Values:

Calories 220, fat 10, fiber 8, carbs 20, protein 16

Chicken Thighs and Rice

Preparation Time: 35 minutes

Servings: 4

Ingredients:

- Chopped carrots: 3
- Chicken thighs: 3 pounds boneless and skinless
- Wine vinegar: ½ cup
- Minced garlic cloves: 4
- Salt
- Black pepper
- Olive oil: 4 tbsp
- Garlic powder: 1 tbsp
- Italian seasoning: 1 tbsp
- White rice: 1 cup
- Turmeric powder: 1 tbsp
- Chicken stock: 2 cups

Directions:

1. Mix all the ingredients in a pan while tossing them, cook in the air fryer for 30 minutes at 370°F. Serve hot.

Nutrition Values:

Calories 280, fat 12, fiber 12, carbs 16, protein 13

Glazed Chicken and Apples

Preparation Time: 30 minutes

Servings: 4

Ingredients:

- Apples: 3 sliced and core
- Olive oil: 2 tbsp
- Chopped rosemary: 1 tbsp
- Salt
- Black pepper
- Chicken thighs: 6 skin-on
- Apple cider: 2/3 cup
- Mustard: 1 tbsp
- Honey: 2 tbsp

Directions:

1. Heat greased pan over medium heat, add cider, honey, and mustard then whisk it. Let it simmer.
2. Toss in chicken, apples, salt, pepper, and rosemary, cook in the air fryer for 17 minutes at 390°F. Then serve hot

Nutrition Values: calories 281, fat 11, fiber 12, carbs 28, protein 19

Lemon Chicken and Asparagus

Preparation Time: 20 minutes

Servings: 4

Ingredients:

- Olive oil: 2 tbsp
- Juice from 1 lemon
- Dried oregano: 1 tbsp
- Minced garlic cloves: 3
- Chicken thigh: 1 pound
- Salt
- Black pepper
- Asparagus: ½ pound trimmed and halved
- Zucchini: 1 roughly cubed
- Lemon: 1 sliced

Directions:

1. Mix all the ingredients in a pan, cook for 15 minutes in the air fryer at 380°F. Serve hot.

Nutrition Values:

Calories 280, fat 8, fiber 12, carbs 20, protein 15

Turkey with Fig Sauce

Preparation Time: 40 minutes

Servings: 4

Ingredients:

- Turkey breast: 2 halved
- Olive oil: 1 tbsp

- Garlic powder: ½ tbsp
- Sweet paprika: ¼ tbsp
- Salt
- Black pepper
- Chicken stock: 1 cup
- Melted butter: 3 tbsp
- Chopped shallot: 1
- Red wine: ½ cup
- Chopped figs: 4 tbsp
- White flour: 1 tbsp

Directions:

1. Heat a greased pan over medium heat. Add shallots and cook for 2 minutes. Add garlic powder, paprika, stock, salt, pepper, wine, and the figs then stir and cook for 8 minutes
2. Add flour and stir. Cook for 2 minutes. Turn off the heat. This is the seasoning sauce
3. Use salt and pepper to season the turkey. Drizzle oil over it, cook for 8 minutes each side in the air fryer at 380°F
4. Top it with the sauce and serve hot.

Nutrition Values:

Calories 246, fat 12, fiber 4, carbs 22, protein 16

Simple Garlic and Lemon Chicken

Preparation Time: 25 minutes

Servings: 4

Ingredients:

- Chicken breast: 4 boneless and skinless
- Garlic heads: 4 peeled with cloves separated and cut into quarters
- Lemon juice: 2 tbsp
- Salt
- Black pepper
- Lemon pepper: ½ tbsp
- Avocado oil: 1 ½ tbsp

Directions:

1. Mix all the ingredients in a bowl, cook for 15 minutes in the air fryer at 360°F. Serve hot.

Nutrition Values:

calories 240, fat 7, fiber 1, carbs 17, protein 18

Tarragon Chicken Breasts

Preparation Time: 25 minutes

Servings: 2

Ingredients:

- Chicken breast: 2 skinless and boneless

- White wine: 1 cup
- Soy sauce: ¼ cup
- Minced garlic cloves: 2
- Chopped tarragon sprigs: 8
- Salt
- Black pepper
- Melted butter: 1 tbsp

Directions:

1. Mix chicken, wine, soy sauce, garlic, tarragon, salt, pepper, and the butter in a bowl and let it sit aside for 10 minutes
2. Transfer to a greased pan and cook in the air fryer for 8 minutes each side at 370°F. Serve hot

Nutrition Values:

calories 271, fat 12, fiber 3, carbs 17, protein 15

Chicken and Pear Sauce

Preparation Time: 30 minutes

Servings: 6

Ingredients:

- Ketchup: 3 cups
- Pear jelly: 1 cup
- Honey: ¼ cup
- Smoked paprika: ½ tbsp
- Chili powder: 1 tbsp
- Mustard powder: 1 tbsp
- Salt
- Black pepper
- Garlic powder: 1 tbsp
- Chicken breasts: 6 skinless and boneless

Directions:

1. Using salt and pepper, season the chicken, cook for in the air fryer for 10 minutes at 350°F
2. Heat a greased pan over medium heat. Add pear jelly, honey, smoked paprika, chili powder, mustard powder, garlic powder, Salt, and pepper and whisk then let it cook for 6 minutes
3. Toss the chicken in it and cook for 4 minutes. Serve hot

Nutrition Values:

Calories 283, fat 13, fiber 7, carbs 19, protein 17

Honey Chicken and Dates

Preparation Time: 35 minutes

Servings: 6

Ingredients:

- Whole chicken: 1 cut into medium pieces

- Water: ¾ cup
- Honey: 1/3 cup
- Salt
- Black pepper
- Olive oil: ¼ cup
- Chopped dates: 4

Direction:

1. Simmer the water in a pot over medium heat. Add honey and whisk then take off the heat
2. Use oil to rub the chicken then season it using salt and pepper
3. Place it in the air fryer basket. Cook it in the air fryer for 10 minutes at 350°F
4. Brush the chicken with honey and cook for 6 minutes each side. Serve it hot

Nutrition Values:

Calories 270, fat 14, fiber 3, carbs 15, protein 20

Chicken and Leeks

Preparation Time: 40 minutes

Servings: 4

Ingredients:

- Chicken thigh: 4 bone-in
- Salt
- Black pepper
- Olive oil: 1 tbsp
- Chicken stock: 1 cup
- Leeks: 3 sliced
- Chopped chives: 2 tbsp

Directions:

1. Heat a greased pan over medium heat. Add stock, leeks and carrots and cover it. Let it cook for 20 minutes
2. Using salt and pepper, season the chicken. Rub it with olive oil. Cook it in the air fryer for 4 minutes at 350°F
3. Place the chicken in the leeks mix. Serve it hot.

Nutrition Values:

Calories 237, fat 10, fiber 4, carbs 19, protein 16

Chicken and Yogurt Mix

Preparation Time: 1 hour and 15minutes

Servings: 4

Ingredients:

- Chicken meat: 17 ounces boneless and cubed
- Red bell pepper: 1 de seeded and cubed
- Green bell pepper: 1 de seeded and cubed

- Yellow bell pepper: 1 de seeded and cubed
- Yogurt: 14 ounces
- Salt
- Black pepper
- Cherry tomato: 3 ½ ounces halved
- Grated ginger: 1 tbsp
- Red chili powder: 2 tbsp
- Coriander powder: 2 tbsp
- Olive oil: 2 tbsp
- Turmeric powder: 1 tbsp
- Cumin powder: 2 tbsp
- Mint leaves: 3 torn

Directions:

1. Toss and mix all the ingredients in a bowl. Keep it in the fridge for 1 hour
2. Place them in a pan. Cook them in the air fryer for 8 minutes each side at 400°F. Serve hot

Nutrition Values:

Calories 245, fat 4, fiber 5, carbs 17, protein 16

Air Fried Chicken Wings

Preparation Time: 55 minutes

Servings: 4

Ingredients:

- Chicken wings: 16
- Salt
- Black pepper
- Melted butter: ¼ cup
- Clover honey: ¼ cup
- Minced garlic: 4 tbsp

Directions:

1. Season chicken wings using the salt and pepper then place it in the air fryer basket. Cook for 25 minutes in the air fryer at 380°F then for 5 minutes at 400°Fheat a greased pan over medium heat
2. Add garlic and sauté for 5 minutes. Add salt, pepper, the air fried chicken and the honey then stir and let it simmer for 10 minutes
3. Place the chicken in the pan and let it sit or a few minutes. Serve it hot.

Nutrition Values:

Calories 274, fat 11, fiber 3, carbs 19, protein 15

Tomato Duck Breast

Preparation Time: 25 minutes

Servings: 2

Ingredients:

- Smoked duck breast: 1
- Honey: 1 tbsp
- Tomato paste: 1 tbsp
- Apple vinegar: ½ tbsp

Directions:

1. Toss and mix all the ingredients in a bowl, cook for 10 minutes each side in the air fryer at 370°F.
2. Cut it into halves and serve hot.

Nutrition Values:

Calories 274, fat 11, fiber 3, carbs 22, protein 13

Turkey, Mushrooms and Peas Casserole

Cooking Time: 30 Minutes

Servings: 4

Ingredients:

- 2 lbs. turkey breasts; skinless, boneless
- 1 yellow onion; chopped
- 1 celery stalk; chopped.
- 1/2 cup peas
- 1 cup chicken stock
- 1 cup cream of mushrooms soup
- 1 cup bread cubes
- Salt and black pepper to the taste

Directions:

1. In a pan that fits your air fryer, mix turkey with salt, pepper, onion, celery, peas and stock, introduce in your air fryer and cook at 360 °F, for 15 minutes.
2. Add bread cubes and cream of mushroom soup; stir toss and cook at 360 °F, for 5 minutes more. Divide among plates and serve hot.

Nutrition Values: Calories: 271; Fat: 9; Fiber: 9; Carbs: 16; Protein: 7

Duck Breast with Fig Sauce Recipe

Cooking Time: 30 Minutes

Servings: 4

Ingredients:

- 2 duck breasts; skin on, halved
- 1 tbsp. white flour
- 1 tbsp. olive oil
- 1/2 tsp. thyme; chopped
- 1/2 cup port wine

- 1/2 tsp. garlic powder
- 1/4 tsp. sweet paprika
- 1 cup beef stock
- 3 tbsp. butter; melted
- 1 shallot; chopped
- 4 tbsp. fig preserves
- Salt and black pepper to the taste

Directions:

1. Season duck breasts with salt and pepper, drizzle half of the melted butter, rub well, put in your air fryer's basket and cook at 350 °F, for 5 minutes on each side.
2. Meanwhile; heat up a pan with the olive oil and the rest of the butter over medium high heat, add shallot; stir and cook for 2 minutes.
3. Add thyme, garlic powder, paprika, stock, salt, pepper, wine and figs; stir and cook for 7-8 minutes.
4. Add flour; stir well, cook until sauce thickens a bit and take off heat.
5. Divide duck breasts on plates, drizzle figs sauce all over and serve.

Nutrition Values: Calories: 246; Fat: 12; Fiber: 4; Carbs: 22; Protein: 3

Chicken Thighs and Baby Potatoes

Cooking Time: 40 Minutes

Servings: 4

Ingredients:

- 8 chicken thighs
- 2 tbsp. olive oil
- 1 lb. baby potatoes; halved
- 2 tsp. oregano; dried
- 2 tsp. rosemary; dried
- 2 garlic cloves; minced
- 1 red onion; chopped
- 2 tsp. thyme; chopped.
- 1/2 tsp. sweet paprika
- Salt and black pepper to the taste

Directions:

1. In a bowl, mix chicken thighs with potatoes, salt, pepper, thyme, paprika, onion, rosemary, garlic, oregano and oil.
2. Toss to coat, spread everything in a heat proof dish that fits your air fryer and cook at 400 °F, for 30 minutes; shaking halfway. Divide among plates and serve.

Nutrition Values: Calories: 364; Fat: 14; Fiber: 13; Carbs: 21; Protein: 34

Chicken and Apricot Sauce Recipe

Cooking Time: 30 Minutes

Servings: 4

Ingredients:

- 1 whole chicken; cut into medium pieces
- 2 tbsp. honey
- 1 tbsp. olive oil
- 1/2 tsp. smoked paprika
- 1/4 cup white wine
- 2 tbsp. white vinegar
- 1/4 cup apricot preserves
- 1 ½ tsp. ginger; grated
- 1/2 tsp. marjoram; dried
- 1/4 cup chicken stock
- Salt and black pepper to the taste

Directions:

1. Season chicken with salt, pepper, marjoram and paprika; toss to coat, add oil, rub well, place in your air fryer and cook at 360 °F, for 10 minutes.
2. Transfer chicken to a pan that fits your air fryer, add stock, wine, vinegar, ginger, apricot preserves and honey; toss, put in your air fryer and cook at 360 °F, for 10 minutes more. Divide chicken and apricot sauce on plates and serve.

Nutrition Values: Calories: 200; Fat: 7; Fiber: 19; Carbs: 20; Protein: 14

Creamy Chicken Casserole Recipe

Cooking Time: 22 Minutes

Servings: 4

Ingredients:

- 10 oz. spinach; chopped
- 1/2 cup parmesan; grated
- 1/2 cup heavy cream
- 4 tbsp. butter
- 3 tbsp. flour
- 1 ½ cups milk
- 2 cup chicken breasts; skinless, boneless and cubed
- 1 cup bread crumbs
- Salt and black pepper to the taste

Directions:

1. Heat up a pan with the butter over medium heat, add flour and stir well.
2. Add milk, heavy cream and parmesan; stir well, cook for 1-2 minutes more and take off heat.
3. In a pan that fits your air fryer, spread chicken and spinach.
4. Add salt and pepper and toss.
5. Add cream mix and spread, sprinkle bread crumbs on top, introduce in your air fryer and cook at 350 for 12 minutes. Divide chicken and spinach mix on plates and serve.

Chicken and Garlic Sauce Recipe

Cooking Time: 30 Minutes

Servings: 4

Ingredients:

- 4 chicken breasts; skin on and bone-in
- 1 tbsp. butter; melted
- 1 tbsp. olive oil
- Salt and black pepper to the taste
- 40 garlic cloves; peeled and chopped.
- 2 thyme springs
- 1/4 cup chicken stock
- 2 tbsp. parsley; chopped
- 1/4 cup dry white wine

Directions:

1. Season chicken breasts with salt and pepper, rub with the oil, place in your air fryer, cook at 360 °F, for 4 minutes on each side and transfer to a heat proof dish that fits your air fryer.
2. Add melted butter, garlic, thyme, stock, wine and parsley; toss, introduce in your air fryer and cook at 350 °F, for 15 minutes more. Divide everything on plates and serve.

Nutrition Values: Calories: 227; Fat: 9; Fiber: 13; Carbs: 22; Protein: 12

Duck and Veggies Recipe

Cooking Time: 30 Minutes

Servings: 8

Ingredients:

- 1 duck; chopped in medium pieces
- 1 cup chicken stock
- 1 small ginger piece; grated
- 3 cucumbers; chopped.
- 3 tbsp. white wine
- 2 carrots; chopped
- Salt and black pepper to the taste

Directions:

1. In a pan that fits your air fryer, mix duck pieces with cucumbers, wine, carrots, ginger, stock, salt and pepper; toss, introduce in your air fryer and cook at 370 °F, for 20 minutes. Divide everything on plates and serve.

Nutrition Values: Calories: 200; Fat: 10; Fiber: 8; Carbs: 20; Protein: 22

Duck Breasts and Raspberry Sauce Recipe

Cooking Time: 25 Minutes

Servings: 4

Ingredients:

- 2 duck breasts; skin on and scored
- 1 tbsp. sugar
- 1 tsp. red wine vinegar
- 1/2 cup raspberries
- 1/2 cup water
- 1/2 tsp. cinnamon powder
- Salt and black pepper to the taste
- Cooking spray

Directions:

1. Season duck breasts with salt and pepper, spray them with cooking spray, put in preheated air fryer skin side down and cook at 350 °F, for 10 minutes.
2. Heat up a pan with the water over medium heat, add raspberries, cinnamon, sugar and wine; stir, bring to a simmer, transfer to your blender, puree and return to pan. Add air fryer duck breasts to pan as well; toss to coat, divide among plates and serve right away.

Nutrition Values: Calories: 456; Fat: 22; Fiber: 4; Carbs: 14; Protein: 45

Chicken and Cauliflower Rice Mix Recipe

Cooking Time: 30 Minutes

Servings: 6

Ingredients:

- 3 lbs. chicken thighs; boneless and skinless
- 3 bacon slices; chopped
- 3 carrots; chopped
- 2 bay leaves
- 1/4 cup red wine vinegar
- 4 garlic cloves; minced
- 4 tbsp. olive oil
- 1 tbsp. garlic powder
- 1 tbsp. Italian seasoning
- 24 oz. cauliflower rice
- 1 tsp. turmeric powder
- 1 cup beef stock
- Salt and black pepper to the taste

- **Directions:**

1. Heat up a pan that fits your air fryer over medium high heat, add bacon, carrots, onion and garlic; stir and cook for 8 minutes.
2. Add chicken, oil, vinegar, turmeric, garlic powder, Italian seasoning and bay leaves; stir, introduce in your air fryer and cook at 360 °F, for 12 minutes. Add cauliflower rice and stock; stir, cook for 6 minutes more, divide among plates and serve.

Nutrition Values: Calories: 340; Fat: 12; Fiber: 12; Carbs: 16; Protein: 8

Greek Chicken Recipe

Cooking Time: 25 Minutes

Servings: 4

Ingredients:

- 1 lb. chicken thighs
- 2 tbsp. olive oil
- Juice from 1 lemon
- 1 tsp. oregano; dried
- 3 garlic cloves; minced
- 1/2 lb. asparagus; trimmed
- 1 zucchini; roughly chopped.
- 1 lemon sliced
- Salt and black pepper to the taste

Directions:

1. In a heat proof dish that fits your air fryer, mix chicken pieces with oil, lemon juice, oregano, garlic, salt, pepper, asparagus, zucchini and lemon slices; toss, introduce in preheated air fryer and cook at 380 °F, for 15 minutes. Divide everything on plates and serve.

Nutrition Values: Calories: 300; Fat: 8; Fiber: 12; Carbs: 20; Protein: 18

Marinated Duck Breasts Recipe

Cooking Time: 1 day 15 Minutes

Servings: 2

Ingredients:

- 2 duck breasts
- 2 garlic cloves; minced
- 6 tarragon springs
- 1 tbsp. butter
- 1/4 cup sherry wine
- 1 cup white wine
- 1/4 cup soy sauce
- Salt and black pepper to the taste

Directions:

1. In a bowl, mix duck breasts with white wine, soy sauce, garlic, tarragon, salt and pepper; toss well and keep in the fridge for 1 day.

2. Transfer duck breasts to your preheated air fryer at 350 °F and cook for 10 minutes; flipping halfway.

3. Meanwhile; pour the marinade in a pan, heat up over medium heat, add butter and sherry; stir, bring to a simmer, cook for 5 minutes and take off heat. Divide duck breasts on plates, drizzle sauce all over and serve.

Nutrition Values: Calories: 475; Fat: 12; Fiber: 3; Carbs: 10; Protein: 48

Chicken Breasts with Passion Fruit Sauce

Cooking Time: 20 Minutes

Servings: 4

Ingredients:

- 4 chicken breasts
- 4 passion fruits; halved, deseeded and pulp reserved
- 1 tbsp. whiskey
- 2-star anise
- 2 oz. maple syrup
- 1 bunch chives; chopped
- Salt and black pepper to the taste

Directions:

1. Heat up a pan with the passion fruit pulp over medium heat, add whiskey, star anise, maple syrup and chives; stir well, simmer for 5-6 minutes and take off heat.
2. Season chicken with salt and pepper, put in preheated air fryer and cook at 360 °F, for 10 minutes; flipping halfway. Divide chicken on plates, heat up the sauce a bit, drizzle it over chicken and serve.

Nutrition Values: Calories: 374; Fat: 8; Fiber: 22; Carbs: 34; Protein: 37

Duck Breasts And Mango Mix Recipe

Cooking Time: 1 hour 10 Minutes

Servings: 4

Ingredients:

- 4 duck breasts
- 3 garlic cloves; minced
- 2 tbsp. olive oil
- 1½ tbsp. lemongrass; chopped.
- 3 tbsp. lemon juice
- Salt and black pepper to the taste

For the mango mix:

- 1 mango; peeled and chopped
- 1 ½ tbsp. lemon juice
- 1 tbsp. coriander; chopped
- 1 red onion; chopped
- 1 tsp. ginger; grated
- 3/4 tsp. sugar
- 1 tbsp. sweet chili sauce

Directions:

1. In a bowl, mix duck breasts with salt, pepper, lemongrass, 3 tbsp. lemon juice, olive oil and garlic; toss well, keep in the fridge for 1 hour, transfer to your air fryer and cook at 360 °F, for 10 minutes; flipping once.
2. Meanwhile; in a bowl, mix mango with coriander, onion, chili sauce, lemon juice, ginger and sugar and toss well.
3. Divide duck on plates, add mango mix on the side and serve.

Nutrition Values: Calories: 465; Fat: 11; Fiber: 4; Carbs: 29; Protein: 38

Chicken and Chestnuts Mix Recipe

Cooking Time: 22 Minutes

Servings: 2

Ingredients:

- 1/2 lb. chicken pieces
- 1 small yellow onion; chopped
- 2 tsp. garlic; minced
- 2 tbsp. soy sauce
- 4 tbsp. water chestnuts
- 2 tbsp. chicken stock
- 2 tbsp. balsamic vinegar
- 2 tortillas for serving
- A pinch of ginger; grated
- A pinch of allspice; ground

Directions:

1. In a pan that fits your air fryer, mix chicken meat with onion, garlic, ginger, allspice, chestnuts, soy sauce, stock and vinegar; stir, transfer to your air fryer and cook at 360 °F, for 12 minutes. Divide everything on plates and serve.

Nutrition Values: Calories: 301; Fat: 12; Fiber: 7; Carbs: 24; Protein: 12

Duck and Cherries Recipe

Cooking Time: 30 Minutes

Servings: 4

Ingredients:

- 4 duck breasts; boneless, skin on and scored
- 1 tbsp. ginger; grated
- 1 tsp. cumin; ground
- 1/2 tsp. clove; ground
- 2 cups cherries; pitted
- 1/2 cup sugar
- 1/4 cup honey
- 1/3 cup balsamic vinegar
- 1/2 cup yellow onion; chopped

- 1/2 tsp. cinnamon powder
- 4 sage leaves; chopped
- 1 tsp. garlic; minced
- 1 jalapeno; chopped
- 2 cups rhubarb; sliced
- Salt and black pepper to the taste

Directions:

1. Season duck breast with salt and pepper, put in your air fryer and cook at 350 °F, for 5 minutes on each side.
2. Meanwhile; heat up a pan over medium heat, add sugar, honey, vinegar, garlic, ginger, cumin, clove, cinnamon, sage, jalapeno, rhubarb, onion and cherries; stir, bring to a simmer and cook for 10 minutes.
3. Add duck breasts; toss well, divide everything on plates and serve.

Nutrition Values: Calories: 456; Fat: 13; Fiber: 4; Carbs: 64; Protein: 31

Chicken Breasts and BBQ Chili Sauce Recipe

Cooking Time: 30 Minutes

Servings: 6

Ingredients:

- 6 chicken breasts; skinless and boneless
- 2 cups chili sauce
- 2 cups ketchup
- 1 cup pear jelly
- 1/4 cup honey
- 1 tsp. garlic powder
- 1/2 tsp. liquid smoke
- 1 tsp. chili powder
- 1 tsp. mustard powder
- 1 tsp. sweet paprika
- Salt and black pepper to the taste

Directions:

1. Season chicken breasts with salt and pepper, put in preheated air fryer and cook at 350 °F, for 10 minutes.
2. Meanwhile; heat up a pan with the chili sauce over medium heat, add ketchup, pear jelly, honey, liquid smoke, chili powder, mustard powder, sweet paprika, salt, pepper and the garlic powder; stir, bring to a simmer and cook for 10 minutes. Add air fried chicken breasts; toss well, divide among plates and serve.

Nutrition Values: Calories: 473; Fat: 13; Fiber: 7; Carbs: 39; Protein: 33

Tea Glazed Chicken Recipe

Cooking Time: 40 Minutes

Servings: 6

Ingredients:

- 6 chicken legs
- 6 black tea bags
- 1/4 tsp. red pepper flakes
- 1 tbsp. olive oil
- 1/2 cup pineapple preserves
- 1/2 cup apricot preserves
- 1 cup hot water
- 1 tbsp. soy sauce
- 1 onion; chopped
- Salt and black pepper to the taste

Directions:

1. Put the hot water in a bowl, add tea bags, leave aside covered for 10 minutes; discard bags at the end and transfer tea to another bowl.
2. Add soy sauce, pepper flakes, apricot and pineapple preserves, whisk really well and take off heat.
3. Season chicken with salt and pepper, rub with oil, put in your air fryer and cook at 350 °F, for 5 minutes.
4. Spread onion on the bottom of a baking dish that fits your air fryer, add chicken pieces, drizzle the tea glaze on top, introduce in your air fryer and cook at 320 °F, for 25 minutes. Divide everything on plates and serve.

Nutrition Values: Calories: 298; Fat: 14; Fiber: 1; Carbs: 14; Protein: 30

Chicken and Radish Mix Recipe

Cooking Time: 40 Minutes

Servings: 4

Ingredients:

- 4 chicken things; bone-in
- 1 tbsp. olive oil
- 3 carrots; cut into thin sticks
- 6 radishes; halved
- 2 tbsp. chives; chopped
- 1 cup chicken stock
- 1 tsp. sugar
- Salt and black pepper to the taste

Directions:

1. Heat up a pan that fits your air fryer over medium heat, add stock, carrots, sugar and radishes; stir gently, reduce heat to medium, cover pot partly and simmer for 20 minutes.

2. Rub chicken with olive oil, season with salt and pepper, put in your air fryer and cook at 350 °F, for 4 minutes. Add chicken to radish mix; toss, introduce everything in your air fryer, cook for 4 minutes more, divide among plates and serve.

Nutrition Values: Calories: 237; Fat: 10; Fiber: 4; Carbs: 19; Protein: 29

Cider Glazed Chicken Recipe

Cooking Time: 24 Minutes

Servings: 4

Ingredients:

- 6 chicken thighs; bone in and skin on
- 1 sweet potato; cubed
- 2 apples; cored and sliced
- 1 tbsp. olive oil
- 1 tbsp. rosemary; chopped.
- 2/3 cup apple cider
- 1 tbsp. mustard
- 2 tbsp. honey
- 1 tbsp. butter
- Salt and black pepper to the taste

Directions:

1. Heat up a pan that fits your air fryer with half of the oil over medium high heat, add cider, honey, butter and mustard, whisk well, bring to a simmer, take off heat, add chicken and toss really well.
2. In a bowl, mix potato cubes with rosemary, apples, salt, pepper and the rest of the oil; toss well and add to chicken mix.
3. Place pan in your air fryer and cook at 390 °F, for 14 minutes. Divide everything on plates and serve.

Nutrition Values: Calories: 241; Fat: 7; Fiber: 12; Carbs: 28; Protein: 22

Duck Breasts with Red Wine and Orange Sauce Recipe

Cooking Time: 45 Minutes

Servings: 4

Ingredients:

- 2 duck breasts; skin on and halved
- 2 cups chicken stock
- 2 cups orange juice
- 2 tsp. pumpkin pie spice
- 2 tbsp. olive oil
- 2 tbsp. butter
- 1/2 cup honey

- 2 tbsp. sherry vinegar
- 4 cups red wine
- Salt and black pepper to the taste

Directions:

1. Heat up a pan with the orange juice over medium heat, add honey; stir well and cook for 10 minutes.
2. Add wine, vinegar, stock, pie spice and butter; stir well, cook for 10 minutes more and take off heat.
3. Season duck breasts with salt and pepper, rub with olive oil, place in preheated air fryer at 370 °F and cook for 7 minutes on each side.
4. Divide duck breasts on plates, drizzle wine and orange juice all over and serve right away.

Nutrition Values: Calories: 300; Fat: 8; Fiber: 12; Carbs: 24; Protein: 11

Veggie Stuffed Chicken Breasts Recipe

Cooking Time: 25 Minutes

Servings: 4

Ingredients:

- 4 chicken breasts; skinless and boneless
- 2 tbsp. olive oil
- 3 tomatoes; chopped
- 1 red onion; chopped
- 1 zucchini; chopped
- 1 tsp. Italian seasoning
- 2 yellow bell peppers; chopped
- 1 cup mozzarella; shredded
- Salt and black pepper to the taste

Directions:

1. Mix a slit on each chicken breast creating a pocket, season with salt and pepper and rub them with olive oil.
2. In a bowl, mix zucchini with Italian seasoning, bell peppers, tomatoes and onion and stir.
3. Stuff chicken breasts with this mix, sprinkle mozzarella over them, place them in your air fryer's basket and cook at 350 °F, for 15 minutes. Divide among plates and serve.

Nutrition Values: Calories: 300; Fat: 12; Fiber: 7; Carbs: 22; Protein: 18

Duck and Tea Sauce Recipe

Cooking Time: 30 Minutes

Servings: 4

Ingredients:

- 2 duck breast halves; boneless
- 3/4 cup shallot; chopped

- 2 ¼ cup chicken stock
- 1 ½ cup orange juice
- 3 tsp. earl gray tea leaves
- 3 tbsp. butter; melted
- 1 tbsp. honey
- Salt and black pepper to the taste

Directions:

1. Season duck breast halves with salt and pepper, put in preheated air fryer and cook at 360 °F, for 10 minutes.
2. Meanwhile; heat up a pan with the butter over medium heat, add shallot; stir and cook for 2-3 minutes.
3. Add stock; stir and cook for another minute.
4. Add orange juice, tea leaves and honey; stir, cook for 2-3 minutes more and strain into a bowl.
5. Divide duck on plates, drizzle tea sauce all over and serve.

Nutrition Values: Calories: 228; Fat: 11; Fiber: 2; Carbs: 20; Protein: 12

Chicken and Peaches Recipe

Cooking Time: 40 Minutes

Servings: 6

Ingredients:

- 1 whole chicken; cut into medium pieces
- 3/4 cup water
- 1/3 cup honey
- 1/4 cup olive oil
- 4 peaches; halved
- Salt and black pepper to the taste

Directions:

1. Put the water in a pot, bring to a simmer over medium heat, add honey, whisk really well and leave aside.
2. Rub chicken pieces with the oil, season with salt and pepper, place in your air fryer's basket and cook at 350 °F, for 10 minutes.
3. Brush chicken with some of the honey mix, cook for 6 minutes more, flip again, brush one more time with the honey mix and cook for 7 minutes more.
4. Divide chicken pieces on plates and keep warm.
5. Brush peaches with what's left of the honey marinade, place them in your air fryer and cook them for 3 minutes. Divide among plates next to chicken pieces and serve.

Nutrition Values: Calories: 430; Fat: 14; Fiber: 3; Carbs: 15; Protein: 20

Chicken and Creamy Veggie Mix Recipe

Cooking Time: 40 Minutes

Servings: 6

Ingredients:

- 29 oz. chicken stock
- 2 cups whipping cream
- 40 oz. chicken pieces; boneless and skinless
- 3 tbsp. butter; melted
- 1/2 cup yellow onion; chopped.
- 3/4 cup red peppers; chopped
- 1 bay leaf
- 8 oz. mushrooms; chopped
- 17 oz. asparagus; trimmed
- 3 tsp. thyme; chopped.
- Salt and black pepper to the taste

Directions:

1. Heat up a pan with the butter over medium heat, add onion and peppers; stir and cook for 3 minutes.
2. Add stock, bay leaf, salt and pepper, bring to a boil and simmer for 10 minutes.
3. Add asparagus, mushrooms, chicken, cream, thyme, salt and pepper to the taste; stir, introduce in your air fryer and cook at 360 °F, for 15 minutes. Divide chicken and veggie mix on plates and serve.

Nutrition Values: Calories: 360; Fat: 27; Fiber: 13; Carbs: 24; Protein: 47

Duck Breasts Recipe

Cooking Time: 25 Minutes

Servings: 4

Ingredients:

- 4 duck breasts; skinless and boneless
- 4 garlic heads; peeled, tops cut off and quartered
- 2 tbsp. lemon juice
- 1/2 tsp. lemon pepper
- 1 ½ tbsp. olive oil
- Salt and black pepper to the taste

Directions:

1. In a bowl, mix duck breasts with garlic, lemon juice, salt, pepper, lemon pepper and olive oil and toss everything.
2. Transfer duck and garlic to your air fryer and cook at 350 °F, for 15 minutes. Divide duck breasts and garlic on plates and serve.

Nutrition Values: Calories: 200; Fat: 7; Fiber: 1; Carbs: 11; Protein: 17

Chicken and Spinach Salad Recipe

Cooking Time: 22 Minutes

Servings: 2

Ingredients:

- 2 chicken breasts; skinless and boneless
- 2 tsp. parsley; dried
- 1/2 tsp. onion powder
- 1 avocado; pitted, peeled and chopped
- 1/4 cup olive oil
- 1 tbsp. tarragon; chopped.
- 2 tsp. sweet paprika
- 1/2 cup lemon juice
- 5 cups baby spinach
- 8 strawberries; sliced
- 1 small red onion; sliced
- 2 tbsp. balsamic vinegar
- Salt and black pepper to the taste

Directions:

1. Put chicken in a bowl, add lemon juice, parsley, onion powder and paprika and toss.
2. Transfer chicken to your air fryer and cook at 360 °F, for 12 minutes.
3. In a bowl, mix spinach, onion, strawberries and avocado and toss.
4. In another bowl, mix oil with vinegar, salt, pepper and tarragon, whisk well, add to the salad and toss. Divide chicken on plates, add spinach salad on the side and serve.

Nutrition Values: Calories: 240; Fat: 5; Fiber: 13; Carbs: 25; Protein: 22

Duck Breasts with Endives Recipe

Cooking Time: 35 Minutes

Servings: 4

Ingredients:

- 2 duck breasts
- 1 tbsp. sugar
- 1 tbsp. olive oil
- 6 endives; julienned
- 2 tbsp. cranberries
- 8 oz. white wine
- 1 tbsp. garlic; minced
- 2 tbsp. heavy cream
- Salt and black pepper to the taste

Directions:

1. Score duck breasts and season them with salt and pepper, put in preheated air fryer and cook at 350 °F, for 20 minutes; flipping them halfway.
2. Meanwhile; heat up a pan with the oil over medium heat, add sugar and endives; stir and cook for 2 minutes.

3. Add salt, pepper, wine, garlic, cream and cranberries; stir and cook for 3 minutes. Divide duck breasts on plates, drizzle the endives sauce all over and serve.

Nutrition Values: Calories: 400; Fat: 12; Fiber: 32; Carbs: 29; Protein: 28

Chicken and Capers Recipe

Cooking Time: 30 Minutes

Servings: 2

Ingredients:

- 4 chicken thighs
- 3 tbsp. capers
- 4 garlic cloves; minced
- 1/2 cup chicken stock
- 1 lemon; sliced
- 4 green onions; chopped
- 3 tbsp. butter; melted
- Salt and black pepper to the taste

Directions:

1. Brush chicken with butter, sprinkle salt and pepper to the taste, place them in a baking dish that fits your air fryer.
2. Also add capers, garlic, chicken stock and lemon slices, toss to coat, introduce in your air fryer and cook at 370 °F, for 20 minutes; shaking halfway. Sprinkle green onions, divide among plates and serve.

Nutrition Values: Calories: 200; Fat: 9; Fiber: 10; Carbs: 17; Protein: 7

Chicken and Black Olives Sauce Recipe

Cooking Time: 18 Minutes

Servings: 2

Ingredients:

- 1 chicken breast cut into 4 pieces
- 2 tbsp. olive oil
- 3 garlic cloves; minced
- For the sauce:
- 1 cup black olives; pitted
- 2 tbsp. olive oil
- 1/4 cup parsley; chopped
- 1 tbsp. lemon juice
- Salt and black pepper to the taste

Directions:

1. In your food processor, mix olives with salt, pepper, 2 tbsp. olive oil, lemon juice and parsley, blend very well and transfer to a bowl.

2. Season chicken with salt and pepper, rub with the oil and garlic, place in your preheated air fryer and cook at 370 °F, for 8 minutes. Divide chicken on plates, top with olives sauce and serve.

Nutrition Values: Calories: 270; Fat: 12; Fiber: 12; Carbs: 23; Protein: 22

Classic Chicken Salad Recipe

Cooking Time: 20 Minutes

Servings: 4

Ingredients:

- Boneless, skinless and halved chicken breast-1 lb.
- cubed feta cheese; -1/2 cup
- lemon juice-2 tbsp.
- mustard-1½ tsp.
- olive oil-1 tbsp.
- red wine vinegar-1 ½ tsp.
- minced anchovies; -1/2 tsp.
- Minced garlic-3/4 tsp.
- water-1 tbsp.
- lettuce leaves; cut into strips-8 cups
- grated parmesan-4 tbsp.
- Cooking spray
- Salt and black pepper to the taste

Directions:

1. Start by Spraying chicken bosoms with cooking oil,
2. Season chicken with salt and pepper.
3. Introduce chicken in your air fryer's bushel and cook at 370 °F, for 10 minutes; flipping the chicken midway.
4. Move the chicken bosoms to a cutting load up, shred utilizing 2 forks, put in a plate of mixed greens bowl and blend with lettuce leaves.
5. Mix feta cheddar with lemon juice, olive oil, mustard, vinegar, garlic, anchovies, water and half of the parmesan In your blender and mix great.
6. Introduce this over chicken blend at that point hurl appropriately, and sprinkle the remainder of the parmesan and serve.

Nutrition Values:

Calories: 312; Fat: 6; Fiber: 16; Carbs: 22; Protein: 26

Chicken & Parsley Sauce

Cooking Time: 55 Minutes

Servings: 6

Ingredients:

- chopped parsley -1 cup
- A drizzle of maple syrup

- chicken thighs-12
- Dried oregano-1 tsp.
- red wine-1/4 cup
- olive oil-1/2 cup
- garlic cloves-4
- A pinch of salt

Directions:

1. In your sustenance processor, blend parsley with oregano, garlic, salt, oil, wine, and maple syrup and shake everything admirably.
2. Mix chicken with parsley sauce in a bowl; hurl well and refrigerate for 30 minutes.
3. Drain chicken, move the chicken your air fryer's crate and cook at 380 °F, for 25 minutes; flipping the chicken once part of the way through the cooking procedure.
4. Carve and share chicken on plates, at that point spread parsley sauce all finished and serve.

Nutrition Values:

Calories: 354; Fat: 10; Fiber: 12; Protein: 17; Carbs: 22;

Quick and Easy Mexican Chicken Recipe

Cooking Time: 30 Minutes

Servings: 4

Ingredients:

- olive oil-1 tbsp.
- salsa verde-16 oz.
- Salt and black pepper to the taste
- boneless and skinless chicken breast-1 lb.
- Chopped cilantro; -1/4 cup
- grated Monterey Jack cheese-1½ cup
- garlic powder-1 tsp.

Directions:

1. Start by Pouring the salsa Verde in a heating dish that accommodates your air fryer, season chicken with salt, pepper, garlic powder.
2. Brush your chicken with olive oil and spot it over your salsa Verde.
3. Preheat your air fryer to380 °F, Introduce the chicken and cook for 20 minutes.
4. Spread cheddar over the chicken and cook for 2 minutes more.
5. Share among plates and serve hot.

Nutrition Values:

Calories: 340; Fiber: 14; Fat: 18; Protein: 18 Carbs: 32;

Tasty Chicken and Lentils Casserole Recipe

Cooking Time: 1 hour 10 Minutes

Servings: 8

Ingredients:

- green lentils-1 ½ cups
- skinless, boneless and chopped chicken breasts; -2 lb.
- chicken stock-3 cups
- minced garlic cloves; -5
- ground cumin; -3 tsp.
- Salt and cayenne pepper to the taste
- chopped yellow onion; -1
- chopped canned tomatoes -14 oz.
- chopped red bell peppers; -2
- Cups corn-2
- Chopped jalapeno pepper-2 tbsp.
- Garlic powder-1 tbsp.
- Cheddar cheese; shredded-2 cups
- chopped cilantro; -1 cup
- Cooking spray

Directions:

1. Put the stock in a dish, include some salt, include lentils; mix, bring to a bubble over medium warmth, spread and stew for 35 minutes.
2. On the other hand; shower chicken pieces with some cooking splash, season with salt, cayenne pepper, and 1 tsp. cumin,
3. Introduce them in your air fryer's bushel and cook them at 370 0for 6 minutes and guarantee you flip midway.
4. Move the chicken to a warmth protected dish that accommodates your air fryer; include chime peppers, garlic, tomatoes, onion, salt, cayenne, and 1 tsp. cumin.
5. Sieve lentils and add them to the chicken blend and hurl everything appropriately.
6. Introduce jalapeno pepper, garlic powder, the remainder of the cumin, corn, half of the cheddar and half of the cilantro,
7. Introduce the chicken into your air fryer and cook at 320 °F, for 25 minutes.
8. Spray the remainder of the cheddar and the rest of the cilantro,
9. Share chicken dish on plates and serve.

Nutrition Values:

Calories: 344; Fat: 11; Fiber: 12; Carbs: 22; Protein: 33

Roasted Chicken Thighs and Baby Potatoes

Cooking Time: 40 Minutes

Servings: 4

Ingredients:

- olive oil-2 tbsp.
- chicken thighs-8
- Chopped thyme-2 tsp.

- halved baby potatoes; -1 lb.
- Dried rosemary-2 tsp.
- Dried oregano-2 tsp.
- minced garlic cloves; -2
- chopped red onion-1
- sweet paprika-1/2 tsp.
- Salt and black pepper to the taste

Directions:

1. mix chicken thighs with potatoes, salt, pepper, thyme, paprika, onion, rosemary, garlic, oregano and oil In a bowl.
2. Toss to coat, spread everything in a heatproof dish.
3. Introduce chicken into your air fryer and cook at 400 °F, for 30 minutes; shaking midway.
4. Share among plates and serve hot.

Nutrition Values:

Calories: 364;Fiber: 13; Fat: 14; Carbs: 21; Protein: 34

Crispy Parmesan Cheese Crusted Chicken Recipe

Cooking Time: 25 Minutes

Servings: 4

Ingredients:

- skinless and boneless chicken breasts -4
- cooked and crumbled bacon slices-4
- Water-1 tbsp.
- whisked egg-1
- avocado oil-1/2 cup
- shredded as iago cheese -1 cup
- grated parmesan cheese-1 cup
- garlic powder-1/4 tsp.
- Salt and black pepper to the taste

Directions:

1. Mix parmesan with garlic, salt, and pepper In a bowl and mix.
2. Get another bowl, put your egg with water in the new pan and whisk well.
3. Start by spicing the chicken with salt and pepper and dunk each piece into egg and after that into the cheddar blend.
4. Introduce your chicken to your air fryer and cook at 320 °F, for 15 minutes.
5. Share chicken on plates
6. Sprinkle bacon and as iago cheddar on top and serve.

Nutrition Values:

Calories: 400; Fiber: 12; Fat: 22; Carbs: 32; Protein: 47

Pan-roasted Japanese Duck Breasts

Cooking Time: 30 Minutes

Servings: 6

Ingredients:

- boneless duck breasts; -6
- Chicken stock-20 oz.
- Soy sauce-4 tbsp.
- Five spice powder-1½ tsp.
- Hoisin sauce-4 tbsp.
- ginger slices-4
- sesame oil-1 tsp.
- Honey-2 tbsp.
- Salt and black pepper to the taste

Directions:

1. mix the five-flavor powder with soy sauce, salt, pepper, and nectar In a bowl and whisk appropriately,
2. Include duck bosoms in the blend, hurl to coat and set aside until further notice.
3. Heat a dish with the stock over medium-high warmth, hoisin sauce, ginger, and sesame oil; blend appropriately and cook for 2-3 minutes more
4. Remove the container from the heat and put aside to cool
5. Put duck bosoms in your air fryer and bake them at 400 °F, for 15 minutes.
6. Share dish among plates, shower hoisin and ginger sauce all over them and serve.

Nutrition Values:

Calories: 336; Fiber: 1; Fat: 12; Carbs: 25; Protein: 33

9 798423 373573